Letters of Madam Guyon

and

A Short Method of Prayer

By

Madam Guyon

(Jeanne Guyon)

Trumpet Press Edition, 2023

Copyright 2023 by Trumpet Press

Author: Madam Guyon (Jeanne Guyon)
Title: Letters of Jeanne Guyon, and A Short Method of Prayer

1. Intimacy with Christ 2. Bible Studies 4. Prayer

ISBN: 978-108-820-147-3

Trumpet Press is a Member of the *Christian Indie Publishing Association* (CIPA).

Book 1:

Letters of Madam Guyon

(also known as Jeanne Guyon)

Book 2:

A Short Method of Prayer

Table of Contents

Book 1:
Letters of Madam Guyon

Preface 7
Sketch of Her Life 8
The Letters 9
Selections From Her Poetry 65

Book 2:

A Short Method of Prayer

Preface To The English Protestant Edition 68

Author's Preface 70

Chapter 1: Prayer Possible at All Times, by The Most Simple 73

Chapter 2: First Degree of Prayer 75

Chapter 3: Second Degree of Prayer 79

Chapter 4: Spiritual Dryness 80

Chapter 5: Abandonment to God 81

Chapter 6: Suffering 82

Chapter 7: Mysteries 84

Chapter 8: Virtue 85

Chapter 9: Perfect Conversion 86

Chapter 10: Higher Degree of Prayer 87

Chapter 11: Rest in The Presence of God 90

Chapter 12: Self-Examination and Confession 92

Chapter 13: Reading and Vocal Prayer 94

Chapter 14: The Faults and Temptations of This Degree 95

Chapter 15: Prayer and Sacrifice Explained 96

Chapter 16: This State Note One of Idleness, But of Action 98

Chapter 17: Distinction Between Exterior and Interior Actions ... 105

Chapter 18: Exhortations to Preachers 109

Chapter 19: Preparation For Divine Union 112

Summary: 118

Letters of Madam Guyon

BEING SELECTIONS OF HER RELIGIOUS THOUGHTS AND EXPERIENCES, TRANSLATED AND RE-ARRANGED FROM HER PRIVATE CORRESPONDENCE

Translated By P. L. UPHAM
(1858)

"Except a corn of wheat fall into the ground and die, it abideth alone; but if it die it bringeth forth much fruit."

PREFACE

Madam Guyon's correspondence was very extensive, occupying five printed volumes. Her style of writing is somewhat diffuse. In giving religious advice to many persons, there would necessarily be frequent repetitions. It has, therefore, occurred to the writer, that a selection and re-arrangement of thoughts, such as is found in this little volume, would be more acceptable and useful, than a literal and full translation of her letters. This selection necessarily involved much re-writing and condensing. Great care, however, has been taken to reach her true sentiments, and to give a just relation of her religious experience.

In the interesting preface to her letters, published in 1767, the writer remarks: "Next to the Holy Scriptures, we do not believe there has been given to the world, any writings, so valuable as Madam Guyon's; and of all these precious treasures, her letters are the most rare. All who have received the unction of the Holy One, whereby they know the truth, are agreed upon her divine writings."

If the writer may be permitted to add her humble testimony, having enjoyed the privilege of reading her writings in the original for several years, she would say, there are no writings, excepting the Sacred Oracles, from which she has received so much spiritual benefit. It is on this account, she has endeavored, with divine assistance, to portray to others, Madam Guyon's deep religious feelings. May the same spirit of devotion to her Lord and Master which she possessed, rest upon the heart of the reader.

Happy are they in whose hearts burns the flame of divine love.

P. L. UPHAM
Brunswick, Me., April, 1858.

SKETCH OF HER LIFE

Jeannie Marie Mothe, the maiden name of Madam Guyon, was born at Montargis, in France, April 13, 1648. She was married to M. J. Guyon, in 1664, and became the mother of four children. In July, 1676, she was separated from her husband by death. Madam Guyon was one of that number, who, in advance of the common standard of piety, are called to be Reformers; and on this account, she suffered great persecutions. She was several times imprisoned. At one time eight months; and subsequently four years in one of the towers of the celebrated Bastile. After her release from prison, she was banished for the remainder of her days to Blois, on the river Loire. At the time of her release from the Bastile, she was fifty-four years of age. Her sufferings from the cold, damp walls of the prison, in winter, and the confined air in summer, with other privations and hardships, greatly impaired her constitution, and rendered her a sufferer to the close of her days. She died June 9, 1717, aged sixty-nine years.

During her imprisonment, she wrote her Autobiography, which has been translated into English. Another work of hers, "The Torrents," has recently been translated, very happily, by Mr. Ford. Also two essays, "Method of Prayer," and "Concise View of the Way of God," by J. W. Metcalf. It is not known by the writer, that her other works have been translated, with the exception of some of her poems by William Cowper; and "The Life and Experience of Madam Guyon," in two volumes, written by my husband. —- P. L. U.

The Letters

REIGN OF CHRIST IN THE HEART

I have read your letter, my dear brother, with great pleasure. It is my highest happiness to see the reign of Jesus Christ extending itself in the hearts of God's people. An external religion has too much usurped the place of the religion of the heart. The ancient saints—Abraham, Isaac, Jacob, Enoch, Job—lived inwardly with God. The reign of Christ on earth is nothing more nor less than the subjection of the whole soul to himself. Alas! the world are opposed to this reign. Many pray, "Thy will be done on earth as it is in Heaven," but they are unwilling to be crucified to the world, and to their sinful lusts. God designs to bring his children, naturally rebellious, through the desert of crucifixions—through the temptations in the wilderness, into the promised land. But how many rebel, and choose rather to be bond-slaves in Egypt, than suffer the reductions of their sensual appetite.

Since Jesus Christ appeared on earth, there is a general belief that the kingdoms of this world will ultimately be subject to his dominion. But we may ask, who hastens his coming, by now yielding up his own heart to his entire control?

Our Lord imposed no rigorous ceremonies on his disciples. He taught them to enter into the closet; to retire within the heart; to speak but few words; to open their hearts, to receive the descent of the Holy Spirit.

The holy Sabbath has not only an external, but a deeply spiritual meaning. It symbolizes the rest of the holy soul, in union with God. Oh! that all Christians might know the coming of Jesus Christ in the soul! Might live in God, and God in them!

God alone knows how much I love you.

TURN FROM SELF TO CHRIST

You are not forgotten, my dear E. God has engraved you on my heart. If you have not consented to the thoughts that have crossed your mind, do not be afflicted on account of them. The examination and dwelling upon these thoughts, brings them again to life. Be on your guard against everything that entangles you in self. God is a Father who bears with the innocent faults of his children, and wipes away the stains they have contracted. The greatest wrong you can do to God is to doubt his love. He regards the simplicity and purity of the intention. It is right to cherish great self-distrust, to realize your weakness and helplessness; but do not stop here. Confide as much more in God, as you hope less from yourself.

Do not afflict yourself, because you do not at all times realize a sensible confidence in God, and other consoling, happy states. Walk by faith, and not by sight, or positive perception of the good you crave. Let us, my dear E., be closely united, and walk together; not according to the way we might choose, but according to the way God chooses for us.

I love you tenderly.

ASSURANCE

Notwithstanding all that is said to me, my dear M., in opposition to my state, I cannot have one doubt of its reality. There is within me an inward testimony to the truth; so deep, that all the world could not shake it. It is the work of God upon my heart, and partakes of his own immutability. It seems to me that all the difficulties of theologians concerning this state, arise from viewing it, not in the light of divine truth and power, but in the light of the creature. It is true, the creature, in itself, is only weakness and sin; but when it pleases God to new-create the soul, and make it one with himself, it is then transformed into the likeness of Christ.

Who will dare limit the power of God? Who will say that God, whose love is infinite as it is free, cannot give such proofs of love as he pleases, to his creatures? Has he not the right to love me as he does? Yes, he loves me, and his love is infinite. I do not doubt it. And he loves you, too, dear M., in the same manner. This is eternal love manifested,—the heart of God drawn out,—expressed towards his creature.

In this state, we understand the mutual secrets of the Lover and the beloved. Who will so deny the truth of the Lord, as to question this? When I hold my beloved in my arms, in vain does one assert, "It is not so,—I am deceived." I smile inwardly and say, "My beloved is mine and I am his!" "If we receive the witness of men, how much greater is the witness of God?"

HUMILITY THE EFFECT OF LOVE

I assure you, you are very dear to me. I rejoice very much in the progress of your soul. When I speak of progress, it is in descending, not in mounting. As when we charge a vessel, the more ballast we put in, the lower it sinks, so the more love we have in the soul, the lower we are abased in self. The side of the scales which is elevated, is empty; so the soul is elated only when it is void of love. "Love is our weight," says St. Augustine. Let us so charge ourselves with the weight of love, as to bring down self to its just level. Let its depths be manifested by our readiness to bear the cross, the humiliations, the sufferings, which are necessary to the purification of the soul. Our humiliation is our exaltation. "Whosoever is least among you shall be the greatest," says our Lord.

I love you, my dear child, in the love of the Divine Master, who so abased himself by love! Oh! what a weight is love, since it caused so astonishing a fall, from heaven to earth,—from God to man! There is a beautiful passage in the Imitation of Christ, "Love to be unknown." Let us die to all but God.

DIVINE COMMUNICATIONS

God communicates himself to pure souls, and blesses, through them, other souls, who are in a state of receptivity. All these little rills, which water others, little compared with the fountain from which they flow, have no determinate choice of their own, but are governed by the will of their Lord and Master. The nature of God is communicative. God would cease to be God if he should cease to communicate himself, by love, to the pure soul. As the air rushes to a vacuum, so God fills the soul emptied of self.

The seven blessed spirits around the throne, are those angels who approach nearest to God, and to whom he communicates himself the most abundantly. St. John, perhaps, was better prepared than any of the apostles to receive the Word, incarnate, dwelling in the soul.

On the bosom of Jesus,—in close affinity with him,—John learned the heights and depths of divine love. It was on this account our Lord said to his mother, "seeing the disciple stand by whom he loved, Woman behold thy Son." He knew the loving heart of John would give her a place in his own home.

God communicates himself to us in proportion as we are prepared to receive him. And in proportion as he diffuses himself in us, we are transformed in him, and bear his image. O, the astonishing depths of God's love! giving himself to souls disappropriated of self, becoming their end, and their final principle, their fullness, and their all.

JOY IN PERSECUTIONS

I am very grateful to you, my dear sir, for your sympathy in my apparent ills. God has not permitted that I should consider them otherwise than blessings. I trust what appears to destroy the truth will, in the end, establish it. Those who maintain the inward reign of the Holy Spirit will yet suffer many persecutions. There is nothing of any value but the love of God, and the accomplishment of his will. This is pure and substantial happiness. This joy no man taketh from us.

It is my only desire to abandon myself into the hands of God, without scruples, without fears, without any agitating thoughts.

Since I am there, O Lord, how can I be otherwise than happy? When divine Love has enfranchised the soul, what power can fetter it? How small the world appears to a heart that God fills with himself! I love thee, my Lord, not only with a sovereign love, but it seems to me I love thee alone, and all creatures only for thy sake. Thou art so much the soul of my soul, and the life of my life, that I have no other life than thine. Let all the world forsake me; my Lord, my Lover lives, and I live in him. This is the deep abyss where I hide myself in these many persecutions. O, abandonment! blessed abandonment! Happy the soul who lives no more in itself, but in God. What can separate my soul from God? Surely, none can pluck me from my Father's hands. All is well, when the soul is in union with him.

LIBERTY IN CHRIST

"If the Son make ye free, ye shall be free indeed." When the man of sin is destroyed, and the new man established in the soul, it finds itself in perfect liberty. As a bird let loose from its cage, the soul goes forth, unfettered, to dwell in the immensity of God. The natural selfish life restricts the soul at every point; and even God, the great I am, is unseen, or deprived of his glory.

When Paul asked, "Who shall deliver me from this body of death?" he added, "I thank God, through Jesus Christ our Lord." That is, when by the grace of God, the new man is established in my soul, I shall be delivered. And, subsequently, when deliverance came, he cried out in transport, "I live, and yet not I. Christ liveth in me!" He was now no more occupied of himself, but let Jesus Christ live and act in him; he was animated by him, as the body is of the soul. If another soul animated our body, the body would obey this new soul; it would become the moving-spring of its operations. Thus Jesus Christ becomes the life of the new man. And what can be more free, more enlarged, than the soul of Jesus? His nature is divine, eternal, boundless. Alas! to what a narrow point does self reduce us! Who that looks at the freedom and expansion of the soul, as it puts on the new man, Christ Jesus, will not crush the reptile self to the dust, that the life of God may again, as in its first creation, animate the soul?

This liberty is as the eagles' wings, of which the prophet speaks, which carries the soul on high. The dove that lighted on Jesus, was an emblem, not only of innocence, but of freedom,—of liberty of spirit to soar and dwell in God. May it please God to give you an experience of this liberty. Quit self, and you will find the freedom and enlargement of the All in All.

MELANCHOLY AVOIDED

I assure you, my dear M., I sympathize deeply in your sufferings; but I entreat you, give no place to despondency. This is a dangerous temptation,—a refined, not a gross temptation of the adversary. Melancholy contracts and withers the heart, and renders it unfit to receive the impressions of grace. It magnifies and gives a false coloring to objects, and thus renders your burdens too heavy to bear. Your ill-health and the little consolation you have from friends, help to nourish this state. God's designs, regarding you, and his methods of bringing about these designs, are infinitely wise.

There are two methods of serving little children. One is, to give them all they want for present pleasure. Another is, to deny them present pleasure for greater good. God is a wise Father, and chooses the best way to conduct his children.

A sad exterior is more sure to repel than attract to piety. It is necessary to serve God, with a certain joyousness of spirit, with a freedom and openness, which renders it manifest that his yoke is easy; that it is neither a burden nor inconvenience.

If you would please God, be useful to others, and happy yourself, you must renounce this melancholy disposition. It is better to divert your mind with innocent recreations, than to nourish melancholy. When I was a little child, a nephew of my father's, a very godly man, who ended his days by martyrdom, said to me, "It is better to cherish a desire to please God, than a fear of displeasing him." Let the desire to please God, and honor him, by an exterior all sweet, all humble, all cordial and cheerful, arouse and animate your spirit:

For this I pray. Ever yours.

GOD'S CARE OF THE SOUL COMMITTED TO HIM

O, that you could realize, my dear friend, how much God loves you. As a painter draws upon his canvas what image pleases him, so God is now preparing your soul, by these inward crucifixions, to draw upon it his own likeness, He cherishes you as the mother her only son. He would have you yield readily to his will, even as the branches of the tree are moved by the light breath of the wind. In proportion to your abandonment to God, he will take care of you. When you yield readily to his will, you will be less embarrassed to discern the movements of God. You will follow them naturally, and be led, as it were, by the providencies of God. God will gently arrest you if you mistake. God has the same right to incline and move the heart as to possess it. When the soul is perfectly yielding, it loses all its own consistency, so to speak, in order to take any moment the shape that God gives it; as water takes all the form of the vases in which it is put, and also all the colors. Let there be no longer any resistance in your mind, and your heart will soon mingle in the ocean of love; you will float easily, and be at rest.

POWER OF THE ADVERSARY

I am deeply afflicted that so many, at the present day, and even some good persons, allow themselves to be openly seduced by the Evil One. Has not our Lord warned us against "false prophets, and the lying wonders of the last days?" All true prophets have spoken in the name of the Lord— "Thus saith the Lord." Nothing gives the enemy greater advantage than the love of extraordinary manifestations. I believe these external movements are a device of the evil one, to draw away souls from the Word of God, and from the interior tranquil way of faith.

The tendency of all communications from God, is to make the soul die to self. An eminent saint remarks, that she had often experienced illuminations from the angel of darkness, more pleasing, more enticing, than those that came from God. Those delusory manifestations, however, leave the soul in a disturbed state, while those that come from God humble, tranquillize and establish the soul in Him. The most dangerous seductions are those, which assume the garb of religion and have the semblance of truth.

Elias appeared alone among four hundred prophets of Baal. These prophets were much agitated, attracting great attention, "crying aloud," etc.

When Elias was told by the angel, that he would see the Lord in Mount Horeb, he hid himself in a cave. He saw a great trembling of the earth. God was not there. There came a great whirlwind. God was not there. Then there came a little zephyr. God was in the still small voice.

The only true and safe revelation, is the internal revelation of the Lord Jesus Christ in the soul. "My sheep hear my voice." This involves no disturbance of our freedom, of the natural operations of the mind; but produces a beautiful harmonious action of all the powers of the soul. I beseech you, my friend, in the name of the Lord, to separate yourself from all these delusions of the adversary.

UNCTION OF GRACE

Friday morning, the 15th, I suffered very much, on account of the individual, whom you know. It seemed to me, that God wished that the all of self in him should be destroyed. I perceived, that although the truths be uttered, proceeded from the inward work of the spirit upon his heart, his reasoning faculty operated so powerfully, without his perceiving it, that the effect of these truths was in some degree lost. Souls are won more by the unction of grace—by the weapons of love—than by the power of argument.

Are not the truths you utter, my friend, too much elaborated by the intellect, and polished by the imagination? Their effect seems to be lost, for want of simplicity and directness. They fall pleasantly on the ear, as a lovely song, but do not reach and move the heart. There is a lack of unction. Are you not always laboring for something new and original, thus exhibiting your own powers of mind, rather than the simple truth?

Receive this suggestion, and light will be given you upon it. Do I speak too plainly? To speak the truth, and the truth only, is all I desire. I have this morning prayed, rather to be taken out of the world, than to disguise the truth. I have proclaimed it, in its purity, in the great Congregation, and it will be seen that Thou, O Lord, hast distilled it in my heart; or rather, O Sovereign Truth, that Thou art there thyself, to manifest thyself plainly, and that Thou dost make use of weak things to confound the strong. God is truth and love. In Him yours.

SPIRITUAL ONENESS

My union with you, my dear child, is steadily increasing. I bear you in my heart with a deep and absorbing interest, and seem anxious to communicate to you the abundant grace poured into my own soul. How close, how dear is the union of souls, made one in Christ! Our Savior beautifully expressed it, when he said, "Whosoever shall do the will of my Father, the same is my mother, sister and brother." There is no union more pure, more strong, than the union of souls in Christ! In this manner, pure as delightful, the saints in Heaven possess each other in God;—a union which does not interrupt the possession of God, although it is distinct from God.

Let your soul have within it, a continual Yes. When the heart is in union with God, there is no Nay,—it is Yes, be it so, which reverberates through the soul. This Yes, this suppleness, renders the heart agreeable to the heart of the Spouse. It was thus with Mary, the mother of our Lord, when the angel messenger came to her, she replied, "Behold, the handmaid of the Lord, be it unto me according to thy word." It was thus with the child-like soul of Samuel, when he said, "Speak, Lord, for thy servant heareth." It was thus with our divine Lord, "Lo, I come to do thy will."

Yours in the fellowship of the Saints.

VICISSITUDES IN EXPERIENCE

As the outgoings of life proceed from the living man, while we live in ourselves, we have a strong will and eager desires, and many fluctuating states. But in proportion as our will passes into the will of God, the desires which are the offspring of the will, are subjugated, and the soul is reduced to unity in God.

As the soul advances in the life of God, its natural or selfish movements decrease; and it depends less on mere emotional exercises, and there is really less variation of the emotions.

Rest assured, it is the same God who causes the scarcity and the abundance, the rain and the fair weather. The high and low states, the peaceful and the state of warfare, are each good in their season. These vicissitudes form and mature the interior, as the different seasons compose the year. Each change in your inward experience, or external condition, is a new test, by which to try your faith and love; and will be a help towards perfecting your soul, if you receive it with love and submission.

Leave yourself therefore in the hands of Love. Love is always the same, although it causes you often to change your position. He who prefers one state to another, who loves abundance more than scarcity, when God orders otherwise, loves the gifts of God more than God himself.

God loves you; let this thought settle all states. Let him do with us as with the waves of the sea, and whether he takes us to his bosom, or casts us upon the sand, that is, leaves us to our own barrenness, all is well.

For myself, I am pleased with all the Lord orders for me. I hold myself ready to suffer, not only imprisonment but death; perils everywhere—perils on the land—perils on the sea—among false brethren; all is good in Him, to whom I am united forever.

PATIENCE WITH THE FAULTS OF OTHERS

I love you very much, my dear M. If my love could be of any avail, it would console you, for I feel a greater tenderness and sympathy for you, than I am able to express. I am more certain than ever, that God designs you for himself. Live exteriorly with N., as being entirely reconciled. Make not too much account of his coldness, his passionate temper, his contempt. It is not by these you are to regulate your conduct, but by a motive more elevated—God and his glory. Let your heart endure his bitterness, for the love of Him, who preferred grief to pleasure. At the same time, do no violence to your own sacred feelings, to accommodate yourself to him, in order to give him a pleasure he cannot appreciate. Regard your present condition, as a means God has given you, to manifest your love to himself, by a willingness to sacrifice yourself. Reject not this cross, shall I not rather say crown, and let all be accomplished between God and your soul, in such a quiet manner, that the struggle with your own feelings will not be perceived.

While you are bearing this daily cross—this real crucifixion—I am certain God will sustain you, from the fullness of his love. All is alike good, when God is with us. I love you tenderly. God loves you; let this make amends for all. In Him devotedly yours.

HOW TO DISTINGUISH THE MOVEMENTS OF GOD

You enquire, how one who desires to follow the movements of God's spirit, may distinguish these movements, from the natural operations of the mind. There is not, at all times, a positive certainty regarding divine movements. If it were so, we should become infallible as the angels; that is, if we were as pure in our intentions. We must walk with God, in entire abandonment and uncertainty, at the risk of sometimes making mistakes, which in the infancy of experience is unavoidable. He who wishes for a particular inspiration, or direction in common matters, which his own reason and judgment can determine, is liable to deception.

A pure soul acts in simplicity, and without certainty, being persuaded that what is good comes from God, and what is not good from self. The greater the simplicity,—the more separate from the mingling of self-activity—the purer are these operations; because the soul in this state is only a simple instrument, that the Word, which is in her, moves, so that it is the Word which speaks and not herself. This manner of speaking, relates to matters of importance, and not to the minute concerns of every-day life. The divine Word, in all exigencies, is found in the soul, that is wholly consecrated to Christ. "When they bring you before magistrates and kings, etc., it shall be given you in that hour what ye shall speak." This method of divine leading—by the hour and by the moment—leaves the soul always free and unencumbered, and ready for the slightest breath of the Lord. This breath, in the pure soul, is as the gentle zephyr, and not as the whirlwind, which shakes the earth. Do not then expect to have anticipated movements, or movements beforehand from God. I have an experience of many years, that God often makes known his will, only in the time of action.

If a pure soul, wholly sacrificed to God, should undertake something contrary to the will of God, it would feel a slight repugnance, and desist at once. If one does not feel this repugnance, let the act be performed in simplicity. A mother who holds her child by a leading-string, loosens it, that it may walk; but if about to make a misstep, she draws the string. The repugnance which a holy soul feels to do a thing, is as when the mother draws the leading-string.

STATE OF SIMPLICITY

I experienced recently, a marked perception of your state, as one in which God took delight, and upon which he had infinite designs, regarding himself and his glory. I saw clearly the state to which God desired to bring you—the means to be used, and the obstacles in the way—the mutual sympathy and confidence he required between us—and the openness and freedom of communication necessary for our mutual benefit, and that we should not hesitate to speak freely of each other's faults.

The peculiarity you remark in my experience, needs some explanation. You say I do not seem to be wounded, nor blame myself when reproved for a fault. To which I reply simply, there is no more of self remaining in me to be wounded. This indifferent state you notice in me, arises from the state of innocence and infancy in which I find myself. Our Lord holds me so far removed from myself, or from my natural state, that it is impossible for me to take a painful view of myself. When a fault is committed by me, it leaves no traces on the soul; it is as something external, which is easily removed. Do not infer that I am blind to my faults. The light of truth is so subtle and penetrating, that it discovers the slightest fault. Souls which are in the natural life, have real faults, as a paper written over with ink is strongly marked, therefore they see and feel them. But souls, transformed into God, have faults, as a writing traced on sand when the wind is high, the wind defacing it as soon as it is traced. This is the economy of divine wisdom, relating to souls in union and harmony with God. Oh! the greatness and simplicity of the way of Truth! How unlike the world's apprehension of it!

QUENCHING THE SPIRIT

Desiring to follow closely the divine leading, I expressed to you the other day, some sentiments you were not able to receive. I perceived at once, that on account of your resistance, I could say no more. From this experience, although painful as regards yourself, I learnt the extreme delicacy of the spirit that seeks to aid others; and the strength of man's freedom to oppose this operation. I realized, also, my inability to act of myself; for, as soon as the spirit in me was silent, I had nothing to say. I had, however, the extreme satisfaction of knowing, that this good spirit alone conducted me; and that I would not, in the least degree, add, nor diminish from its operations.

It was from a knowledge, gained by experience, of the extreme delicacy and purity of this divine spirit, that I remarked to you, the other day, that if you did not receive the instructions I then imparted, I should have nothing farther to communicate to you. O, how pure and how unlike the impetuous operation of man's spirit, is this operation of God!

SUFFER THE CRUCIFIXIONS AND REDUCTIONS OF SELF

All the graces of the Christian, spring from the death of self. Let us, then, bear patiently the afflictions, which reduce this overflowing life. There is a suffering in connection with confusions and uncertainties, very trying to bear. Unbounded patience is necessary, to bear not only with ourselves, but with others, whose various tempers and dispositions are not congenial with our own. "Offenses,"—wounds of spirit will occur while we live in the flesh. These offenses must be borne in silence, and thus subjugated and controlled by the spirit of grace. By a law of our nature, we feel, more or less, the influence of the spheres in which we move.

While we honor, we think, the true cross, the affliction that comes from God, let us remember, that these instruments, so disagreeable, are the true cross that providence daily furnishes us.

Do not sully the cross and mar its operations, by your murmurs and reflections. Let us welcome any trials, that teach us what we are, and lead us to renounce ourselves and find our all in God.

Jesus Christ says, "He who renounces not all that he hath, cannot be my disciple." Of all possessions, that of ourselves is the most dangerous.

Please present my cordial regards to your brother. I sympathize deeply in his misfortunes. I use this expression, in conformity to common usage, but it does not express the sentiments of my heart. I am convinced that the loss of wealth, worldly honor, persecutions, are the best instruments to unite us to Jesus Christ. All evils, or apparent evils, are great blessings when they unite us to our All in All. I pray God, to sustain him.

His sufferings only increase my sympathy and love for him in our Lord. My health is still feeble, but all is well in the depths of my heart. God is there.

REPROVE IN LOVE

It is important to use great care and sweetness in reproving others. Reprove only when alone with the person, and take not your own time, but the moment of God. As we are not free from faults ourselves, we must not expect too much from others. Be yourself very humble and child-like, and this character will act sympathetically on others. Jesus Christ was full of sweetness and charity. How patiently did he bear with his imperfect disciples, even with Judas, without anger, without bitterness, and even without coldness.

How lowly was Jesus! He "did not break the bruised reed." He imparts to his little ones no tyrannic power. They use no violence in dealing with souls, but say with John, "Behold the Lamb of God, who taketh away the sins of the world." Our Lord, "rejoiced in spirit," in an unusual manner, such as we find nowhere else in Scripture, when he said, "I thank thee, O Father, Lord of heaven and earth, because thou hast hid these things from the wise and prudent, and revealed them unto babes." How happy are we in the presence of a little child; how much at ease! It imposes on us no burden of restraint, of fear, of management! It is in this childlike disposition of meekness, of sweetness, of innocence, that we should seek to benefit others.

In the love of Jesus, yours.

SILENT OPERATION OF GRACE

I perceive, by your letter, you are in doubt about the grace which passes inwardly from heart to heart. We notice an illustration of this in the woman who touched our Lord, when he said: "I perceive that virtue is gone out of me." In a similar manner, without words, one heart may communicate grace to another heart, as God imparts grace to the soul. But if the soul is not in a state to receive it, the grace of the interior is not communicated, as is expressed in another passage; "If they are not children of peace, your peace will return to you again." This illustrates, according to my view, pure interior communications of the grace of God, from heart to heart, which the soul relishes in silence, and which silence is often more efficacious than a multitude of words.

At our last interviews I had an inclination for silence, but finding in you an aversion to silent communion, I entered into conversation, but without any interior correspondence on my part, and, evidently, without any benefit to you. God would teach you, my dear child, there is a silence of the soul through which he operates, filling it with the unction of grace, to be diffused on other hearts who are in a state of receptivity, often more efficacious than words to replenish the soul.

We find this still harmonious action in nature. The sun, the moon, and stars, shine in silence. The voice of God is heard in the silence of the soul. The operation of grace is in silence, as it comes from God, and may it not reach and pass from soul to soul without the noise of words? O, that all Christians knew what if means to keep silence before the Lord!

LIMIT NOT YOUR SPHERE

Let me urge you, my child, to enlarge your heart; or, rather, suffer it to become enlarged by grace. This contraction shuts you up in yourself, and hinders an agreeable openness which we should ever maintain, even towards those who have no particular affinity with ourselves. An open, frank exterior wins confidence. Let it not appear, that you have so much relish for yourself, as not to think of others. What seems to us a virtue is sometimes regarded by God as a fault; and which we shall so perceive, when we have clearer light.

You seem to mark out for yourself a certain sphere, and if you go beyond it, you think you do yourself an injury. Thus, while you have an apparent movement, you are only describing a circle, whose center and circumference is self. I entreat you, pass beyond the narrow bounds of self;—suffer yourself to be led out of self into the will and way of God. Thus you will be much more happy and useful. If I loved you less, I should be less severe.

Let God be the sovereign Master over our hearts, and instruct, and reprove, and operate in us, by himself, or through others, as pleases him.

Adieu. God bless you, my child.

SECRET OF DIVINE OPERATIONS UPON THE SOUL

Do not suppose, Dear Sir, that you are to be purified by great trials and extraordinary events. All is accomplished in you by the suppleness of your will,—by the state of infancy. It must be so on account of the pride of your natural reason. God conducts the soul in a way opposed to human philosophy. Hence the necessity of being reduced to the state of infancy, and to the subjection of the will. What we call the death of the will, is the passage of our will into the will of God. This change implies not only a change in externals, but the inward subjection of the desires and sentiments of the heart. Here most persons, who commence the religious life, stop short. They cannot submit to the interior crucifixion, which lays prostrate the whole of the natural carnal life, and consequently there follows a mingling of the spirit of the flesh with grace, and it is this which produces such monsters in the religious world. Do we not read in Scripture, that in consequence of the alliance of the sons of God with the daughters of men, giants were born, who so filled the earth with wickedness, they drew down a deluge of wrath upon the world? It is from this abominable alliance of the flesh with the spirit, that all those who appear in the world, as "mighty men, men of renown," are produced and sustained. One may be full of the natural life, while apparently dead to the external things of the world. Thus they are dead to inferior things, and alive in the most essential points—dead in name, but not in reality.

By an authority as gentle as efficacious, God accomplishes his will in us, when we have surrendered our souls to him. The consent we give to his operations, and our relish of them, is sweet and sustaining, in proportion to the perfection of our abandonment. God does not arrest the soul with violence. He adjusts all things in such a manner, that we follow him happily, even across dangerous precipices. So good is this Divine Master, so well does he understand the methods of conducting the soul, that it runs after him, and makes haste to walk in the path he orders.

Suppleness of soul is, therefore, of vital consequence to its progress. It is the work of God to effect this. Happy are the souls, who yield to his discipline. God renders the soul, in the commencement, supple to follow illuminated reason; afterwards to follow the way of faith. He then conducts the soul by unknown steps, causing it to enter into the wisdom of Jesus Christ which is so different from all its former experience, that without the testimony of divine filiation, which remains in the soul in a manner hidden, and the ease and liberty the soul finds in this unknown way, it would consider itself as being separated continually from God, being left, as it were, to act of itself. Human wisdom being here lost, and the powers of the soul controlled by the wisdom of Jesus Christ, born in the soul, it increases in its proportions, even unto the stature of a perfect man in Christ Jesus.

The soul, having now passed into God, is in its proper place, and will be happy, provided it remains fixed and separate from its former manner of acting.

Reason may at times oppose with all its strength, and cause some fears, some hesitations; but, being fixed in God, it is impossible for the soul to change its course; and, after the experience of many useless sufferings, having their origin in self, it suffers itself to be drawn in the current of love. There is now no more of violence to nature. The soul is in its natural state. The ease and naturalness of this state causes, at times, some fear, some anxiety. It is as much the nature of man, originally, and in his new creation in the likeness of Christ, to be in God, and to be there in perfect enlargement, simplicity, and innocence, as it is the nature of water to flow in its channel. When man is as he should be, his state is one of infinite ease and without limitations, because he is created sovereign, or master of himself, and cannot be subjected by anything created, although he is subjected to God, if that may be called subjection, which brings the soul into affinity with God, and makes it partaker of his nature.

Be therefore persuaded, that God uses no violence in dealing with the soul. This commotion in the soul, arises from the resistance of man's will to divine operations. When the soul is disenfranchised of all that is opposed to the will of God; when it is not arrested either by desires or repugnancies, it runs without stopping or weariness in the way. This is what is called death,—death to self; but the soul was never so much alive; it now lives the true life, the life of God.

When the soul becomes one with God by the loss of its own will and life, it has purposes, and it is important to follow them; but they are purposes in God, and have in them nothing of self. All that has rapport to self is no more, and God is all. Being passed into God, the soul is changed and transformed in him. This is what the mystics call Resurrection. But the word used in this way, does not bear its usual signification. To resuscitate is to revive the former life. But in this case, the will, or natural life is consumed, and gives place to the will or life of

God. Thus the Holy Spirit operates effectively in the soul, transforming it into the likeness of the Son of God.

Now the soul participates in the qualities of God, one of which qualities, is that of communicating itself to other souls. Or rather, it is as a stream, which, being lost in a large river, follows the course of the river, communicating itself where the river communicates, watering where it waters, drawing into itself all the smaller rivers, which are destined alike to lose themselves in the great ocean of Love. These streams have no independent life, but proceed from, and flow back into their origin. Here is the consummation of souls in oneness, as Jesus Christ has expressed it,— "One in us."

There is divine reality in this truth. Blessed are those who comprehend it! How many walk side by side along these rivers, and yet never mingle their waters! And many there are, also, who haste with eagerness, to precipitate themselves into this divine stream, and flow together, as the souls of the celestial ones, in the fullness of divine love.

This is not a chimera of the fancy; it is the wonderful economy of divinity. It is the end and object of the creation of the soul—the end and compass of all the efforts of God, regarding his creatures. Here is consummated all the glory, God derives from their existence. All beside are only the means approaching this final end, this glorious termination, and absorption of the soul in Deity. Here is the light which ravishes the soul. A light which does not precede, but follows the soul in its progress; unfolding more and more, as a man in a dark cavern, discovers the concealed places, only when he has remained in it for some time.

This is the pure Theology in which God instructs the angels and the saints. It is the Theology of Experience, that God teaches only to his children, who having abandoned their own wisdom, he has himself become their wisdom and their life. This is the law of wisdom, my friend, for us,—the way of the

Lord in us. In him we are one.

NO UNION WITH SELFISH SOULS

There are some souls which cause me great suffering. These are selfish souls, full of compromises, speculations and human arrangements, and desiring others to accommodate themselves to their humors and inclinations. I find myself unable to administer in the least degree to their self-love; and when I would be a little complaisant, a Master, more powerful than myself, restrains me. I cannot give such persons any other place in my heart, than God gives them. I cannot adapt myself to their superficial state, neither respond to their professions of friendship; these are very repulsive to my feelings.

The love which dwells in my heart, is not a natural love, but arises from a depth which rejects, what is not in correspondence with it, or rather what is not in unison with the heart of God. I cannot be with a child without caressing it, nor with a child-like soul without a tender attachment. I do not regard the exterior, but the state of the soul; its affinity and oneness with God. The only perfect union, is the union of souls in God; such as exists in heaven, and on earth after the resurrection, life takes effect in the soul.

NEVER YIELD TO DISCOURAGEMENT

Do not be disheartened, my friend, on account of your slow progress. A long martyrdom is sometimes necessary, in order to purify our souls from the concealed faults of self-love—faults interwoven in our nature, and strengthened by long indulgence. As you cannot control at once the agitations of nature, arm yourself with patience, to accomplish the task little by little; not in the way of direct effort, but rather by ceasing from effort, remaining quiet, permitting neither gestures nor words to betray your feelings.

Could we enter into the highest state of grace, as we enter into a room, it might be easily accomplished. But alas! the door is straight, and there are many deaths to pass; in a word, death to self. It is this long martyrdom, or dying of the old man of sin, which causes all the pains of the interior life. It is rare to find persons, who are willing to die entirely to self, and therefore few reach the highest state of grace.

Have good courage. It is a great work to draw a large ship from her moorings, but when she is in the waters, how easily she rolls! What happiness, when by perseverance, you have triumphed over nature, to find yourself in the abundant waters of grace! I pray God to put his own hand to the work. He will.

In Him, devotedly yours.

WEAKNESS AND IMPERFECTION

I reciprocate your friendship, madam, with all my heart. Our divine Master knows how happy I am to serve you in any possible way. Oh! madam, it is better to be feeble, when God leaves us in our weakness, than to have a strength which is our own. I once thought, that the pure soul was free from all faults, but I now see otherwise. God clothes his children with frailties, that they may be humble in their own eyes, and be concealed from the eyes of the world. The Tabernacle was covered with the skins of the beasts, while the Temple of Herod was ornamented with gold. Let us not afflict ourselves on account of our littleness and infirmities, since God so orders it, but become as little children. When a little child falls, it cannot raise itself, but lets another do for it all that it needs.

It does not depend on ourselves to make the presence of God more or less sensible. Let the desire for a lively sense of this presence, be crucified to the will of God. Take what is given you. Be as the little child, who eats and sleeps and grows. God gives you the best nourishment, although not always the sweetest to the taste. Adieu! my heart sympathizes with you.

ADVANCEMENT

During the process of the soul's purification and advancement, it loses sight not only of itself, but of all things else; except God; and even of the distinct apprehension of our Lord, in his humanity. That is, there are no longer distinct, bounded views and perceptions of Christ, the soul becoming identical with Christ. This is necessary in order to draw the soul into oneness with God. Let all go in the divine order. When the soul has returned to its end and origin, and is lost in God, it finds all it lost, without going out from God.

When the soul is yet in itself, it draws all things to itself, and sees God and all creatures in itself. But when the soul is in oneness with God, it carries all creatures with it in God, and sees nothing separate from God. Seeing all in God, it sees all things in the true light, as with the eye of God. This is what David calls, "Seeing light in thy light."

May God give you understanding of what I say, and docility and acquiescence in the truths, which he causes to penetrate your soul. I make no reserves, but express freely all my thoughts. The least reserve for self, is as a strong breath against a mirror, it obstructs the view of God. My soul, it seems to me, is clear and transparent, reflecting only what the Master presents; and the execution of his will renders the soul always increasingly pure and transparent. May God be all in all to you.

GREATNESS OF SPIRITUAL POVERTY

Do not measure yourself by others, who may not be led as you are. God chooses to enrich some souls with brilliant gifts, but he has chosen you, stripped of all, in the depths of spiritual poverty. This is the perfect self-renouncement, without which, one cannot be the disciple of the Lord Jesus. All other states, however elevated they may be, are inferior to this pure, naked state of the soul. It is a state, which despoils the lover of all he possesses in favor of his Beloved. It is a state in which the soul is shielded from all inroads of the enemy; who can reach only what remains of self in the creature, and not what is enclosed in God.

God has chosen you for himself alone. You are the sanctuary, which is open only to the high priest, in which is contained the ark of the covenant—the essential, will of God—the sacred place, encompassed by the clouds, where the glory of God appears. Oh! blessed poverty of spirit, in which state the soul is enriched with the best gifts a God can bestow!

Measure not your advancement by relation to the road passed over, but by rapport to the end. There yet remains a great road to pass over, since God himself is the way.

The more fully you enter into his designs, the more I love you.

ASSISTANCE RENDERED BY ONE SOUL TO ANOTHER

The interest I feel in your spiritual welfare, my dear F., is very great—so deeply absorbing, that I slept but little during the past night, presenting you in prayer before our Lord. I have an inward conviction, that God is enriching your heart by my humble instrumentality; thus, while he elevates you on one side, he debases you on the other, by communicating his grace through so unworthy a channel as myself. The Spirit has revealed to me your state, when I have received no intelligence from you. God has thus ordered it, for his own glory; and when many years hence, this method of God's operations will be better known—the assistance rendered by one soul to another, without the mediation of the body—the use he has made of this feeble instrument to communicate to you his grace, will serve to substantiate this divine truth and heavenly mode of operation.

There is therefore for you, a means of interior advancement, which no distance of place can interrupt. It will be only from lack of correspondence on your part, that it will be diverted. God desires it, at least for a time, until your soul is entirely in union with himself. This method of communication is only a superior fountain discharging itself into another; or, as two rivers bearing each other to the same sea.

Receive then this poor heart in the fullness of Christ's love, and believe me, no one can be more fully united to you than I am.

SIMPLICITY AND POWER OF THE WORD

You enquire, my friend, why I do not use obscure terms and extraordinary expressions, in explaining the Scriptures. My Lord teaches me, that while there are no writings so profound as the Gospels, there are none so simple. And further, that simplicity of soul gives simplicity of expression. When we speak of a state beyond our experience, we do so with difficulty, and have recourse to learning to aid us, and use forced expressions.

In the natural, simple expressions of Scripture, there are deep sentiments, adapted to the wants of each soul—to those less and more advanced.

The word of God enters the center of the soul; it has a penetrating quality; an operative efficiency. No words of man can produce the same effect; at least, none but such as come from souls, who are pure channels of the word of God. It is the good pleasure of our Lord, to express and reproduce himself upon the self-abandoned soul. Who does not admire the profound mystery of the creation of the world, where God produced all things by his word? When God created man, he formed him of the dust of the earth—the lowest form of matter—made of dust, that he might not rob God of his glory! But man thus created, received the spirit—the breath of the Word. This dust of the earth became the living breath of God. When Jesus Christ is formed in the soul, he imparts not only a clear understanding of the word, but is himself the Word, reproduced in the soul. Those only in whom Christ dwells, fulfill the word, or have the word accomplished in them. Such only are able fully to interpret the word. It is not learning which best explains the truths of God, but the reproduction of these truths in the life—-the experience of them.

FORGETFULLNESS OF SELF

I cannot compliment you, dear sir, and I am persuaded, that you will expect from me, only the simplicity of the Christian. This simplicity leads me to say, only what our Lord gives me. You need more of this simplicity. The frequent self-returns you make, dwelling so much on your unworthiness, although it may have the appearance of humility, is only a refined self-love. True simplicity regards God alone; it has its eye fixed upon him, and is not drawn towards self; and it is as pleased to say humble as great things.

All our uneasy feelings and reflections, arise from self-love, whatever appearance of piety they may assume. The lack of simplicity inflicts many wounds. Go where we will, if we remain in ourselves, we shall carry everywhere our sins and our distresses. If we would live in peace, we must lose sight of self, and rest in the infinite and unchangeable God. These self-returns have a tendency to establish the soul more and more in itself, and hinder it from running into its great original. But it is to this, God is calling you. You withhold from God the only thing he desires—the possession of your heart. The time is short; wherefore spend it in the compass and surroundings of self? The single eye sees only God. You act as a person who being called before a king, instead of regarding the king and his benefits, is occupied only with his own dress and appearance. God wishes to disarrange you—to destroy self; and you wish to preserve what he would destroy. Be more afraid of self than of the evil one. It is the spirit of Satan to exalt self above God, and this spirit is fostered by these continual returns you make upon your own doings and misdoings, which leaves no place in your mind for the occupation of God.

DIVERSITY OF MEANS OF SANCTIFICATION

Although there are impenetrable mysteries in God's dealings with souls, in order to promote their sanctification, it is true that each soul, aside from the ordinary means, common to all, has a specific training, and this method of the divine order can alone accomplish the work. The means that sanctifies another may not sanctify you. You, my friend, will not be led by great crosses and severe sufferings, but in the way of helpless infancy. The child-like, yielding soul is necessary for you; therefore God has chosen a child, myself, to be your helper. Forget yourself as the man to whom many eyes are turned, and become the little, helpless one, who cannot take care of itself, but lets another care for it. The pride, presumption and vanity, of the natural man, must give place to the littleness and simplicity of the child. Says our Savior, "Except ye be converted, and become as little children, ye cannot enter into the kingdom of heaven." O, when shall we learn that it is littleness, and not greatness, that God requires of his child!

God has given me a maternal yearning for your soul. I sympathize deeply in your wants and burdens. Be assured, the eyes of the God of Love are upon you. I entreat you, yield to the influences which are in operation to restore your soul to God. I can offer no apology for my letter; for in all things, I obey my Lord.

COMFORT IN AFFLICTION

I assure you, Dear Sir, I sympathize deeply in your afflictions. With all my heart I present you before our Lord. I have prayed, and still pray, that if you are called to participate in the sufferings of Jesus Christ, you may partake also of his patience and submission. You will find the Lord at all times near your heart, when you seek him by a simple and sincere desire to do and suffer his will. He will be your support and consolation in this time of trouble, if you go to him, not with fear and agitation of spirit, but with calm, confiding love.

Jesus said to the blind man, whose eyes he anointed with clay, "Go wash in the waters of Siloam"—waters soft and tranquil. O, that you might experience the abiding peace which Christ gives. O, that you might become reduced to the simplicity of the little child! It is the child who approaches the nearest to Jesus Christ. It is the child whom he takes in his arms and carries in his bosom. O, how lovely, how attractive, is child-like simplicity! May the sufferings you are now experiencing, render you, child-like and submissive to all the will of your Father. My ill health forbids my writing more fully. God loves you, and you are very dear to me in him. Amen. Jesus, help.

BEARING FRUIT IN UNION WITH CHRIST

God has united my soul to yours in the oneness of his own nature, and when all the obstructions on your part are removed, you will realize this same divine union. "We have many masters, as said St. Paul, but only one Father in Christ." This Father unites himself to us by the impartation of his own nature, and from this communication, of himself to the soul, proceeds our spiritual paternity; or the power by which we communicate to others what we receive from him. We are not always sensible how this power, or aid we render others, is imparted. In some individuals it is more manifest than in others. It always adapts itself to the subject who receives it. All the gifts and graces of the spirit are either more sensible and apparent, or more spiritual and inward, according to the power of receptivity in the individual.

It seems to me that when I am with you, there is only a simple, imperceptible transmission from my soul to yours. You do not perceive any marked results, and they are not great, because you are not in a state to receive much, and often interrupt me by speaking, which causes in me a vacillation of grace. If we were together some considerable time without distraction, you would perceive more marked results. It is the desire of God that there should be, between us, perfect interchange of thoughts, of hearts, of souls;—a flux and reflux, such as there will be when souls are new-created in Christ Jesus. At present, my soul in rotation to yours, is as a river which enters into the sea, to draw and invite the smaller river to lose itself also in the sea.

This truth,—the fruitfulness of souls who are in God, whereby they communicate grace,—however much it is rejected, is, nevertheless, a truth. This flux and reflux of communication, like the ebbing and flowing of the great ocean-current, is the secret of the heavenly hierarchy, and makes a communication from superior orders to inferior,—and of equality, between angels of the same order.

During all eternity, the communication of God the Father, and the Son, to angels and saints, and their reciprocal communication to each other, will be a well-spring of blessedness. The design of God, in the creation of men, has been to associate to himself living beings, to whom he could communicate himself. He could create nothing greater than likenesses of himself. All the splendor of angels and saints, is but light reflected from God.

God could not see himself reflected in saints, without their participating of these two qualities, fruitfulness and reciprocal communication. In this life all perfection consists, in that which makes the consummation of this same perfection in heaven, No one can be perfect, if he is not perfect as the Father in heaven is perfect; that is, partaking of his nature.

Jesus Christ is the Father of souls; his generation, or the souls that are begotten of him, are eternal in their nature as he is. The figure, "giving us his flesh to eat," is the nourishment he gives the soul in communication with himself; or himself reproduced, or begotten in us. The eternal Word is the essential, undying life of the soul.

DESOLATE STATE

Believe me, dear madam, I take a deep interest in your spiritual welfare, and I earnestly hope your confidence in God will not fail, on account of your present desolate state. As the winter plunges still deeper the roots of the trees in the earth, so the wintry state of the soul plunges it deeper in humiliation. Remember the confidence of Job, "Although he slay me, I will trust in him." Although stripped of all consolation, and left in the desolation of nothingness, you may yet rejoice in God—out of, and separate from, self. Let the earth be stripped of her foliage; let neither flowers nor fruit appear; yet God is, therefore you may be happy. The mother loves to sacrifice herself for her child, and finds her life in what affords it happiness; thus die to self, in relation to God.

When your weaknesses rise up before you, when you would weep over some error in judgment, or some unguarded expression, do as the little child, who having fallen into the mud, carries its hands to its mother, who cheerfully wipes them, and consoles him after the fall. Can you not believe God loves you, as much as you love the little one enfolded in your arms? Does he not say, "A mother may forget, yet I will never forget thee!"

The discovery of your weakness and emptiness, is an evidence of God's love; and while it is ground for humiliation, it is also of thanksgiving. When it pleases God to fill this void with his grace, it is cause of thankfulness; but if we realized at all times this fullness, we should be in danger of appropriating the grace of God to ourselves. Thus, our times of desolation are necessary, and we should accept them joyfully, as a portion of the bread our father gives us.

Yours in tender sympathy.

SELF-ABANDONMENT

The death of self is not accomplished at once. It is for some time a living death. Its opposite, spiritual life, is represented by Ezekiel's vision of the dry bones. First, the bones were rejoined; afterwards covered with sinews; then the flesh appeared; and finally, the spirit of the Lord animated them. When the soul begins to incline towards God, it finds many obstructions; but in proportion as we yield to the will of God, these obstructions are removed. The following simile will help to illustrate my idea. The rivers empty themselves into the sea; before they lose themselves there. Wave by wave following its course, seems to urge onward the river, to lose itself in the sea. God imparts to the soul some waves of pure love, to urge on the soul to himself; but as the river does not lose itself in the sea, until its own waters are exhausted, so the soul reaches God, and loses itself in God, only when the means of supply from self are at an end. As the waves, which are precipitated into the sea, roll many times before they are lost in the sea, so the soul undergoes many changes, before it is received into God.

The results of self-crucifixion are happy, because God then becomes all to the soul. We lose self, and substitute God in its place. We take away the finite, and receive the Infinite. This is blessed.

NO DEPENDENCE ON INSTRUMENTS

What shall I say regarding the state in which you find yourself, in relation to me? I have no movement either to promote our re-union, or hinder it. Let God direct. Are you leaning upon him, or upon the creature? If on the creature, it is a bruised reed, which will fail you. God sometimes makes use of instruments, whom he finds it necessary afterwards to reject. If he designs to remove me from you, can I have any wish to retain you? God forbid. He may design this separation, to make you die to any confidence in the creature. He may no longer design to use me for your benefit. I might have mingled my own impurity, with his pure light flowing through me. If God permit me to err, it is on account of my pride. I have never given you any assurance of my infallibility. What am I but an erring creature? Leave me, leave me, and unite yourself only to God, who will never mislead you. Means are good, only in the order of God. They injure us, if we rest in them. If God remove me from you, acquiesce in his will, with a devotion worthy of a child of God. Be humble, and courageous enough to own your fault, in leaning on an arm of flesh. Men of the world may be obstinate, but the child of God should be supple. Whatever separation there may be between us, believe me, you will always be dear to me in our dear Lord. I hope, when you are lost in him, you will find this little drop of water, (myself) in the same great ocean of love.

CHILD OF GOD SOON TO DIE

I have had a presentiment that you would not survive this illness. I lose in you the most faithful, and the only friend on whom I could rely, in the persecutions which threaten me. I feel my loss, but rejoice in your happiness, I could envy you. Death only lends a helping hand to rend away the veil, which hides infinite beauties. Our Lord has strongly cemented our souls. May the benediction of the divine Master rest upon you. Go, blessed soul, and receive the recompense prepared for all those, who are wholly the Lord's. Go, we separate in the name of the Lord; I cannot say a last adieu, for we shall be forever united in him. I hope, in the goodness of God, to be present with you in heart and spirit, at the time of your departure, and to receive with you, the divine Master who is waiting for you. Be my ambassador in the courts above, and say to him I love him.

UNION OF SOULS IN GOD

The assurance you give me of the union of your soul with mine, is a great consolation. It is a union to which my heart fully responds, not in a way of emotional transport, but in the depths of peace; there is nothing of nature in it. It is a union in Jesus Christ. We are one in a sense of our lost condition, and one in self-abandonment. Oh! blessed oneness with Christ, where all evils perish; and there remains only the casualties inseparable from the state of humanity. How wonderful is this operation—the sacred mingling of a poor creature with its God, where all the evils of our fallen nature, are removed from the depths of the soul, and the soul, in its elemental being is lost in its original! There all the little ones are united in Him,—these little drops of water reassembled in the divine ocean! How swiftly do the streams embrace each other, and flow into one channel, when the obstructions are removed! When souls become pure in Jesus Christ, they flow into one another with the same rapidity. Purity of soul consists in an entire separation from self, and re-union with God. The soul can return to self; it has the power, and therefore is not infallible.

Our union, my dear friend, is independent of the relish or dis-relish of all created things and events. You could not be separated from me without being separated from God; for it seems to me, that I am one with him, and inseparable, and you are the same; and thus, we are one in Him, and one with each other.

Ever yours, in the heart of Jesus.

SECRET OPERATIONS OF GRACE

My heart has been tenderly united to you, during all my bodily sufferings. In proportion as the outward man has been reduced, God seems to be more the life of my soul. Although the operations of God upon your soul may be less marked than formerly, they are no less real. There is a secret fire in your heart, which burns continually, although imperceptibly. This keen and continual operation enfeebles you, because it consumes so rapidly the more sensible and marked operations of the soul. This is, I apprehend, your ordinary state; with occasionally the unction of the oil of grace poured upon the concealed fire, to give you a sweet and clear manifestation of the loving presence of God.

You bear two marked results of the divine presence—interior recollection, and a continual amen in your heart; a true and just response to all God's dealings with your soul.

I realize a very close union with you. This union is not in the emotions, and not in the will of man, but in the will of God. It is a union, from which I could no more separate myself, than from God; it is a fulfillment of the prayer of our Lord, "that they may be one, as we are one." It is a union which death cannot interrupt, but will substantiate more and more fully in God.

Ever yours, in our Lord.

TO A YOUNG FRIEND

You are very dear to me, my child. Do not think I have forgotten you. God alone can render you happy. Give yourself wholly to him, never more to take yourself back. Love him with all your heart. Retire often within the closet of your heart to commune with God. Do not pray to him in a constrained and formal manner, but all simple and natural. God loves better the affectionate language of the heart, than, the cold and discursive thoughts of the intellect. The prayer of love softens the heart.

Do not shrink from your ordinary duties. We are often more united to God, in our daily avocations, than in retirement. The reason is, our good Father holds us more closely, when we are most exposed to temptations. Endeavor to maintain, at all times, harmony and oneness with God. You have only to abandon yourself wholly to divine love, and perform all the duties that devolve upon you. Do not be restive, and thus mar God's beautiful design and operation upon your soul. Place in his bosom of rest, all your worries, and allow him to carry you, as a little child is borne by its mother. This little one has only to regard, lovingly, the smiles of its tender mother.

God will give you a wise discernment as to food and drink, and all the pleasures of life. He calls us to a temperate life, but not to a life too austere. We should avoid the too much and the too little in eating and drinking.

I pray our divine Lord, to enlighten, strengthen and comfort your heart.

LETTER TO HER SPIRITUAL GUIDE

The state in which I find myself, my Father, takes away from me entirely, the liberty to address you any longer as my Spiritual Guide. I realize so great a detachment from all things, that there remains in me only a triumphant, dominant love, which acknowledges no master but Love. It is my experience, that the closer the union of the soul with God, the more it is separated from all dependence on the creature. I find also, that the secret operations of divine love upon the soul, cannot be expressed. These operations do not consist in sweet and flattering expressions, neither in consolations, in the ordinary way, but in the discovery of mysterious truths; truths, which give so profound a knowledge of God, that the soul can find no language to give expression to these views.

To speak, and to act, is the same thing with God. "He spake, and it was done." When the divine Word operates in the soul, without any obstruction, the soul becomes what this Word wills it should become. When Mary Magdalene was made whole, it was no more Mary Magdalene, but Jesus Christ, who lived in her. St. Paul says, "I live, yet not I, Christ liveth in me." In the same manner, the Word is incorporated into my soul.

Some time since, there was given me a view of the States of Mary, the mother of our Lord. I was alone in my chamber, and my soul was completely filled with divine love. The divine Word seemed to say within me, "I will show thee the chief work of my hands,—a perfect nothing in itself,—the heart of Mary." In this manner was conveyed to me, the inexpressible love of God for men—his operation in pure souls. It was shown me, that her silence and acquiescence in the will of God; her entire self-crucifixion and hidden life were worthy of imitation; and that this same love which had operated so powerfully upon this soul, emptied of self, desired to draw other souls also to her states, and to make an effusion of the same grace and love in them, as in her. O divine love! how great are thy wonders, how marvellous thy operations on human hearts! My soul is lost in the depths of thy secret wonders! Silence, silence—only silence!

I write to you, my Father, for the last time, to bid you a final adieu. I can no longer listen to any other teachings, than this divine Word of eternal Truth, which is spoken in the depths of my heart. But however far separated from you, in the relation of Director, you are very near and dear in the affections of my heart; in that pure love, which is alone the operation of our Lord Jesus Christ.

GLORY OF GOD THE ONE DESIRE

What have we to desire in heaven and on earth, only the

glory of God? But it is necessary to desire the glory of God as he desires it. He who has absolute power over the heart of man, has a plan of operations; he does all things in their time; he waits until the hour is come. In coming into the world, our Lord could have converted the world at once, and destroyed all its vices; but the economy of his wisdom did not so direct. When I hear our Lord say, "Mine hour is not yet come," and wishing neither to advance nor retard, for a moment, the hour that his Father had appointed, I am plunged into my nothingness. We are only instruments in his hands, which he may lay aside, or use according to his good pleasure. We should be so dead to self, as to be indifferent, whether he makes use of us or not.

Remain, therefore, my dear friend, in the hand of God. Let him accomplish in you, and by you, all his good pleasure, whether to cast down, or build up. God knows how much I love you.

SPIRITUAL UNION AND AID

Spiritual union, is a state of the soul very clear in my perception, although I may not be able to give you a definite impression of this state. In order to benefit you, it became necessary for me to enter into your state, to have an experimental knowledge, an endurance and suffering of the same state. By this experience I have been brought into closer relation to God, partaking more fully of the Christ-like nature by being rendered capable of bearing the infirmities of others. And I have had, also, a clearer idea of that quality of God, whereby he multiplies holy souls, by the communication of himself. In this experience, the soul appears to be in God, and God in her, as first cause, drawing and penetrating the soul nearest to himself, and by penetration, in this soul, drawing, through her instrumentality, many other Souls.

Although, by these powerful rays the soul itself may seem to penetrate and draw other souls, yet it is God who draws them by his efficiency; and he communicates this efficiency, most powerfully, to those in closest contact with himself. So pure and transparent is this soul, that there seems to be no space between the first Mover and the souls moved by the agent or instrumentality. There is a difference between the ray and the body of the sun, although it is difficult to separate the ray from the sun. It is the divine ray, which is transmitted through this soul, as the natural ray through the medium of the atmosphere. These same rays, transmitted through many souls, and from soul to soul, unite them in one common center, and thus the bond of descent is complete in God. I may not express myself so as to be understood. May your light supply, what is wanting in clearness of expression.

LIVE IN THE PRESENT

Do not expect, my dear E., that the will of God will be made apparent to you in any extraordinary way. The most remarkable events occur naturally. It was by an order of the Emperor, that Joseph, being of the house and lineage of David, went to be taxed at Bethlehem, where the holy child Jesus was born. The fountain of water was near to Hagar, when she laid down the child to die with thirst. Behold God, my friend, in the present arrangement of his providence for you, and submit wisely to passing events. He sees the end from the beginning, and plans wisely for his children. O, how good to submit our limited view to his far sight, reaching through time and eternity!

Remember, the present moment comes to you, as the moment of God. Use it for his glory, and every succeeding moment. Thus the present becomes the eternal moment, for which we must render account to God. May God be All in All to us in every passing moment, now and forever.

HOW TO ADMINISTER REPROOF

A single word, spoken in the spirit of Christ, with humility and sweetness, will have more weight, in correcting others, than many words uttered in our own spirit. The reason is this: when passion mingles with correction, although the truth may be spoken, Jesus Christ does not cooperate with us. Therefore, the person is not corrected by what we say, but, being opposed to the manner of correction, is more confirmed in the evil. In proportion as Jesus Christ speaks by us, without us, or without the minglings of self, his word is efficacious, and turns the heart of the person to whom we speak, to receive what we say. I know there are some who resist, knowingly, his word, but our passionate zeal does not correct them.

It is important to wait the moment of God to collect others. We may see real faults, but the person may not be in a state to profit by being told their faults. It is not wise to give more than one can receive. This is what I call preceding the light,—the light shines so far in advance of the person, that it does not benefit him. Our Lord said to his apostles, "I have many things to say to you, but you cannot bear them now."

The prophet says, the Lord carries his children in his arms, as a nurse. A nurse could wish that the child could walk alone, but she waits in patience the time. Let us do the same, and never discourage the weak. Let us not destroy the good grain with the tares. Who does not admire "the long suffering patience of God?" And I may add to St. Paul's words, all unworthy as I am, and of those who admire it, how few imitate it! If those to whom God has given so much grace, have so many faults themselves, with how much patience should they bear with those who are less favored.

BEARING THE STATES OF CHRIST

During my late severe illness, a strong impression rested on my mind, that I was called to participate in the last sufferings of Jesus Christ. The language of my heart was, I am ready, O, Father, to suffer all thy will! In thus yielding my heart, as Abraham when called to sacrifice his beloved Isaac, I realized a new bond of alliance with Christ, and these words, "I will betroth thee unto me forever," was the voice of the Bridegroom to my soul.

When Paul said, "I bear in my body the marks of the Lord Jesus," he did not refer to any external marks in the flesh, but to bearing the states of Jesus Christ. In David are expressed all the states of Christ, with the difference only there is between the type and the original. Job was an eminent instance of being reduced to nothingness, and also of exaltation by the favor of God. Those who pass through the furnace, and suffer with Christ, are prepared to wear the white robe, which adorns the bride, the Lamb's wife. Their souls become the dwelling-place of the Most High.

Are not those beautiful subterranean palaces, which we read of in fable, and which are reached after crossing deep caverns, and so hidden that none can find them, only those to whom the secret is revealed, representative of the interior palace of the soul, where the Lord inhabits. "The king's daughter is all glorious within."

OUR IMPERFECTIONS SHOULD NOT HINDER OUR LABORS FOR OTHERS

Although I am so weak and unworthy in myself, God uses me for the good of others. The many defects of our temperament, should not hinder our labors in behalf of others. These faults have nothing to do with the grace, which operates effectively on the souls for whom we labor. God reveals himself, through the fathers and mothers in Israel, and thus increases confidence in them; while, at the same time, their weaknesses forbid placing too much dependence on them.

Although our Lord acquaints us with his designs regarding others, and the aid we may render them, yet this should not give us the least desire to aid them, only in the order of his providence. Neither should we be arrested in his work, although the souls we aid repulse the effort. God will make good the results in due time. It implies great death to self, never to put our hand selfishly to the work of the Lord, as it does, also, never to go a step out of the path in which he leads us. When we mingle self, we retard, rather than advance, his work. Nature is so corrupt that it deeply infests spiritual things, and so subtle as to conceal itself under all artifices.

I do not know why I have written you thus. God knows, and that is sufficient.

DEATH, RESURRECTION

This is no time to be disheartened. When the sinful lusts rebel, leave them to their disorderly cravings. Let them cry, as a child from whom we take away a dangerous yet pleasing toy. Strengthen yourself for crosses and humiliations. You will soon be made alive in Jesus Christ.

The extraordinary peace you have tasted, is the commencement of the resurrection-life. This peace is not invariable, because the new life is given little by little, yet, I assure you, it will soon fill your whole soul. As God has rapidly advanced inward death, and caused you to run, with a giant step, in the way of self-crucifixion, and this, notwithstanding all the oppositions of the carnal man, he will also thus rapidly advance the resurrection.

The loss, of all things of the earthly life, which follows the resuscitated life, will be deep and extended. The death and burial which precede the resurrection, cannot compare with that total loss, which follows the resuscitated life. This is something different, and in a new state. You will arise from the sepulchre, as the Spouse of the Beloved.

All is consumed in myself, not in the ordinary way, but in a total loss; so that there remains nothing which can be named or known. It seems to me, the death of self is carried almost to infinity, it makes so many unknown steps. Since this morning, this unworthy creature experiences a still greater reduction of self than ever before. Die, live; lose yourself, and find yourself again; then you will have experience of this state.

GRACE DEEPLY INTERIOR

While you perceive nothing sensible, or apparent, in your religious state, there is, at the same time, evidence to others of a hidden spring of life within your soul. God does not give you the sweet rain which, falling, clothes all the surface of the soul with verdure, but he gives you the deep well-spring, by which means you live and flourish, and produce, not herbs and flowers, which are born and die in the same day, but substantial fruits, ripening for eternity. David said, the life of man upon the earth is as grass, which grows up in the morning, and withers in the evening. This refers to the natural life, but it is also true of the selfish life of man. It flourishes in the morning of the spiritual life, but no sooner does the sun of righteousness arise in his warmth, than this life withers and is cut down. The righteous are as a tree planted by the rivers of water, whose leaf is always green. This is because the roots are well watered by the deep-flowing current.

God never ceases to operate in your heart. The calm, resigned state of your soul is proof of this.

Take good care of your health. Do not labor beyond your strength. God will abundantly reward you for your labors of love in behalf of others. These are labors he never fails to recompense. I pray God, my dear F., to preserve you for his work. I have many things to say, but I forbear. Your time is precious.

SELF-RENUNCIATION

God designs you, my friend, for himself, but he will lead you by a way, entirely opposed to what you have marked out. He does this in order to destroy your self-love. This is accomplished only by the overthrow of all your purposes, preconceived views, natural reason and sagacity. Self-love has many hiding-places. God alone can search them out. You seek the honor that cometh from man, and love to occupy a high position. God wishes to reduce you to littleness, and poverty of spirit. Believe me, dear sir, you will grow in grace, not by knowledge acquired from books; not from reasonings upon divine truths, but by an efflux from God. This efflux will reach and fill your soul, in proportion as you are emptied of self. You are so much occupied of yourself in speaking, reading and writing, that you give no place to God. Make room, and God will come in.

You speak of your many cares. If you will give yourself wholly to God, these cares will be greatly diminished. God will think for you, and arrange by his Providence, what you cannot effect by long years of planning. In the name of God, I entreat you to renounce your own wisdom, your self-leadings, and yield up yourself to God. Let Him become your wisdom. You Will then find the place of rest, you so much need.

May you read this letter, with dependence on the Spirit, which has dictated it, and without regard to the instrument, and your heart will testify to the truth of what I have written. Take courage, and be persuaded that if God destroys the natural life, it is only to give you himself. Endeavor to be nothing, that God may be all. When void, God himself fills the space.

UNEXPECTED FAULTS

Yesterday, after I left the parlor, I uttered some words hastily, and suffered very much in consequence; a suffering not like the pangs of penitence I formerly experienced, but more subtle and interior; and the soul was more acquiescent. Whether it was the words I uttered too precipitately, or the reflections that followed, which caused this suffering, I could not determine. A part of myself seemed to be thrown out of God, as we see the ocean reject certain things, which it receives again more deeply into its bosom. Thus I seemed to myself to be rejected, and without any power to make the least movement to return, and without even a regret that I was rejected. I was willing to remain where God placed me, until the moment he received me again to himself. If I should afflict myself on account of this experience, which was new and unexpected, I believe it would be wrong, and sully still more the soul. The depths of my soul remain unchanged—fixed in God. He removes the impurity, that has exteriorly sullied it, and holds the soul still his own.

APOSTOLIC STATE

I have read your letter, my dear F., with great pleasure. The true Apostolic state is to become all things to all men; that is, to impart to each one spiritually, according to his necessities. Only those who are reduced to littleness and simplicity, have this power of communicating grace. They have also the ability to sympathize deeply in the states of others; of bearing in some measure their burdens, and are sometimes in great heaviness on their account. This communication of grace and aid, is not necessarily restricted to the personal presence of the individual. We may be "absent in body, yet present in spirit," after the manner of God's operations; and as the angelic powers communicate to us. It is only by the enlightening of God's Spirit, that we realize the state of those to whom we are spiritually united.

Unity of souls is experienced, not only with those in the body, who have affinity with ourselves, but also with those out of the body. I realize with the holy prophet David, a correspondence and unity, which renders our souls one in God. You will experience this unity with the saints more fully, when all perception of self is taken away. St. Paul says, "Ye are come to an innumerable company of angels—to the spirits of just men made perfect." David was in the Old Testament, what Paul was in the New. They were both deeply interior Christians. The Apostles, after having received the Holy Ghost, spake all languages. This has also a spiritual meaning. They communicated grace, according to the necessities of each one. This is speaking the word—the efficacious word, which replenishes the soul. This nourishing, life-giving word is represented by the manna, and the reality is found in the Lord Jesus Christ, who is himself the bread of life in the soul. Amen, Jesus!

PAINFUL EXPERIENCE

To-day my health is better, and I find myself able to reply to your letter. Let the view of yourself that God gives you, be accepted, whether it relates to your fallen condition in general, or to particular faults; but add nothing to this view by your own reflections. These continual reflex acts of the mind, do not help you; they do not remove the faults. I am not surprised, that you find in yourself so many evils; evils which render you almost insupportable to yourself. When God accomplishes the work of purification, he removes all that is opposed to the divine inflowing life.

These evils of your nature, which are now apparent, and which were deeply concealed, are perceived by you, only because they are passing out from their hiding-places. All persons do not have so deep a knowledge of themselves; therefore do not suffer so much, because all are not destined to so profound a death and burial while in the body. Be silent, and drink the bitter cup. These humiliations will endure until your state is in some degree perfected; after which they will become more and more slight, and only at intervals, until the death and burial is consummated.

ECSTACY OF THE MIND, AND THE WILL OR HEART — THE DIFFERENCE

The intellectual part of man can be in some degree united to God; but the soul loses itself in God, only by the loss of the will and by love. This loss of the will is the true ecstasy, which is a permanent state, and is effected without any violence to nature. When love is the controlling exercise, the will follows, and the soul is reduced to unity; as in the natural exercise of love, the stronger the love, the greater the submission of the soul to the object beloved. Sacred love does not bind parts, but draws it fully, until it is absorbed wholly in this divine oneness.

The mind may tend towards its divine object, with ardor, but the will not concurring, causes dissonance and swooning, or impetuous transports. I call this momentary ecstasy; it cannot long endure without separating the soul from the body.

The difference between these two states is, as that of water, retained in the air by a machine, and of a river, running naturally into the sea, as ordered by the grand Architect of the universe. Love, which carries the will in its train, changes the whole man; this is the divine, the true ecstasy. This is what is called transformation, and loss of the soul in God. It is certain, however, that the creature always remains a being distinct from God.

A VIEW OF SELF

The activity of the natural selfish life, is the greatest obstacle to your progress. Allow of nothing which gives sustenance to this life. Be on your guard against applause. Applaud not yourself when you have done well. Admit no reflections in regard to the good you have accomplished, so that all that nourishes self-complacency may die.

Possess your soul in peace as much as possible; not by effort, but by ceasing from effort; by letting go everything that troubles you. Be quiet, that you may settle, as we leave water to settle when agitated. When you discover your errors and sins, do not stop, under whatever good pretext, to remedy them. Rather abandon yourself at once to God, that he may destroy, in you, all that its displeasing to him. I assure you, you are not capable of yourself, to correct the least fault. Your only remedy is abandonment to God, and remaining quiet in his hands. If you discovered the depth of inward corruption in your heart, your courage would fail! On this account, God conceals from us, in part, the view of our sins, and discovers them to us, only as he destroys them.

Rest assured, God loves you. He will take care of you. Have faith in his love and mercy. You will see farther by and by. When you are in trouble, do not fail to write me. Have good courage, and all will be well. You are very dear to me in our Lord.

STATE OF A SOUL IN UNION WITH GOD

Although, in the latter part of my life, I do not perceive those marked states of abandonment and submission, neither of interior sorrows, such as I formerly experienced, this does not prove that these distinct states no longer exist; but the soul having become more fully established in God, it makes less account of them, or is less affected by external impressions. As pure flowing water leaves no trace where it passes, so these distinct states leave no durable impression. The soul seems to have lost its own qualities of resistance and aversion, and runs, without ceasing into its Original. It is on this account I cannot write so fully of my states of mind as formerly. My soul, in its depths, rests in God. "My peace, says Christ, I give unto you."

I pray for the church; I mourn at times that God is so little known and loved; but these feelings are transient, and the soul is ready to take any impression that God gives it. While it seems to have no consistency of its own, so to speak, it adapts itself to the state of others with wonderful facility. Sometimes even relating amusing stories, to children, and to those who cannot be entertained in any other way.

The soul, in this state of union with God, is sometimes permitted to foretell things to come, which appear very obscure to man, but which are, nevertheless, infallibly true, because proceeding from God. The knowledge of the event, and its full explanation, will come in the fullness of time. The soul is ready for anything; ready for nothing. All that is true comes from God; what is not true, from the creature. The soul does not seek to justify itself, nor produce humiliation, but passes on, disregarding self, and absorbed in God.

STATE OF REST IN GOD

If I do not reply to you, Dear Sir, as soon as you might expect, it is because I hold myself in reserve, until I have a movement to write, and not from any want of regard to you. Relative to the distinct, voluntary acts of resignation, renouncement, it would be difficult, in my present state, to make such acts, because such acts would seem to imply something of self-appropriation still remaining; whereas, I have given to my Sovereign, all that I am; and as far as I know, I have nothing more to give him. My soul is at rest in his will.

It is the same in regard to prayer, or petitions. The soul having a very simple method of prayer, all other prayer seems foreign to it. When it would make a request, and as soon as the soul knows distinctly what it demands, there is something which goes before to accomplish it, without the utterance of words. When the soul utters words, or makes petitions, if the spirit accompanying approves, the prayer is made with ease. If the spirit do not cooperate, the words are uttered with difficulty, or not at all. God takes the place of self in the soul, and there prays for things agreeable to his will. This is a state of the soul, in which it has no desire to originate prayer, but loves to be silent in the presence of God. This is an experience more satisfactory than I am able to express. O, that all the earth knew what it means to keep silence before the Lord!

GREAT HUMILIATIONS

I have a clear discernment of your state. It seems to me, I see it in some measure as God sees it; that is, in the pure light of truth,—the reasons why you suffer, and the blessed results of these sufferings. I have known that the period of discipline would be long, and very long, because you suffer not only on your own account, but also for the benefit of others. God destines you to accomplish great things for his glory, and exterior humiliations in your case not being suited to his designs, he makes use of concealed humiliations, known only to yourself and God. I will repeat to you the words addressed by our Lord to St. Paul. "My grace is sufficient for thee; my strength is made perfect in weakness."

It will be in companionship with humiliations, that you will be saved from falling into sin and error, and be prepared to become a vessel fit for the Master's use. You will experience from time to time, a return of these humiliating states, and when you may think they have entirely passed away, they will suddenly revive. But the greater your humiliation, the more God will use you to perform his most excellent works. In this state of entire self-reduction and humiliation, your words will be clothed with power.

"I am come," says our Lord, "to bring fire on the earth." O martyr of Pure Love, — a sacrifice for the good of others, what if the fires be already kindled in your bosom, shrink not! If you were less to God, he might spare you.

Do not hesitate to speak to me of your sufferings, because it appears to you useless. It is not so. If you speak of them in simplicity, your heart will be relieved, and strengthened. I know how to sympathize with you. God bless you.

REPOSE OF THE SOUL IS GOD

Having given up myself wholly to God, and loving Him far better than myself, how can I find any opposition to his good pleasure? How can I do otherwise than yield to one I love better than myself? How can a soul withdraw from the dominion of a Sovereign, that it loves with the whole heart? "What can separate us from the love of God, in Christ Jesus?" Although, while we remain in this life, there is a possibility of sinning, and of separation from God, and it is true, that the soul remains in oneness with Him, only by the continuance of his mercy, and that if he should leave it, it would immediately fall into sin, yet I cannot have the least fear, that my God will leave me, or that I shall ever separate myself in any degree from his love.

The creature can take no glory to itself, to whatever state it may arrive. O that you might comprehend what I cannot express—the sense I have of the goodness of God, to keep what is his own! How jealous, how watchful he is over the soul! God seems so truly all things to me, that I seem to see nothing, to love nothing, relish nothing, only what he causes me to see, love and relish in himself. I am only capable of loving and submitting to him, so much is he my life. I believe God blindfold, without questioning or reasoning. God is; this is sufficient. How immense is the freedom of the soul in him! O may you not doubt, that when all of self is taken away from the creature, there remains only God. O God, can I have any self-interest, or appropriate aught as mine? In what can I take it? How strange the thought! how far removed from the possession of God! I am lost. God is.

POWER OF CASTING OUT EVIL SPIRITS

Although for many years, profound truths have been revealed to me, and God has manifested his power through me, in an extraordinary manner, my state has invariably been one of infancy, simplicity and candor. God's grace has rendered me equally willing to lie concealed, or to execute his will more publicly. During seven years, without my knowing how it was accomplished, as soon as I have approached some persons, possessed by demons, the evil spirits have departed. I have realized simply a desire to relieve them, and this desire, or prayer, has been answered in a way unknown to myself. Of myself, I have no goodness nor power at all. I have only the capacity of a child—of letting myself be used by God, as pleases Him. My life appears natural. I am encompassed with infirmities. My health is greatly impaired. My infirmities are a balance-wheel, a counterpoise to exaltation. Yet life is ever flowing, without any thought of the means of sustaining it, as we live in the air, without thinking of the air we breathe.

STATE OF A SOUL RE-UNITED TO GOD

In reply to your enquiry, my dear children, concerning my state, I would say, that exteriorly, I am open, simple, childlike. My interior resembles a drop of water, mingling and lost in the ocean, and no more discerning itself,—the sea not only surrounding, but absorbing it. In this divine immensity, the soul discerns and enjoys all objects in God. All is darkness and obscurity in respect to itself; all is light on the part of God. Thus, God is all to me. This has been my state more than thirty years, although in latter years I have realized greater depths in these experiences. Think of the bottomless sea; what is thrown therein, continues sinking, without ever reaching the end. Thus divine love is the weight of the soul, that sinks it deeper and deeper in God. "God is Love, and he who dwells in love, dwells in God, and God in him." O immensity!

Jesus Christ, the embodiment of truth and love, has explained the Scriptures by fulfilling them. So when the soul has passed into God, the Word is fulfilled in the soul, as it was in Christ. O Love! thou art thyself the pure, naked, simple truth, which is expressed, not by me, but by thyself, through me. Amen.

CONCISE VIEW OF THE INTERIOR WAY

The soul seeks God in faith not by the reasonings of the mind and labored efforts, but by the drawings of love; to which inclinations God responds, and instructs the soul, which cooperates actively. God then puts the soul in a passive state, where he accomplishes all, causing great progress, first by way of enjoyment, then by privation, and finally by pure Love.

What do we understand by the Interior way? It is to seek the kingdom of God within us. Luke 17, 21. We find this kingdom only where God has placed it, within the soul. It becomes necessary, then, to withdraw the eyes of the soul from external landmarks and observations, which man, in the pride of reason, has located around it, and rest the eye in faith, on the Word of the Lord,— "Seek and ye shall find." This seeking, involves an interior activity of the soul; a desire, a determination, and searching after what is hidden.

When the soul has thus earnestly sought the kingdom of God within, this kingdom is developed little by little. Interior recollection becomes less difficult, and the presence of God more perceptible and agreeable. Formerly it was supposed, that the presence of God was only the thought of God, and that it was necessary to force the mind—to concentrate the thoughts with violence to find God. This is true in some sense, but, as the soul cannot long endure this tension, and as the kingdom of God is not found in the external vestments of the soul, but in its depths, this labor is of little avail. So little progress is made, the soul becomes discouraged, and the evil one, who fears nothing so much as the reign of God in the soul, makes an effort to draw the soul to external issues.

In order to accomplish this object, he takes two methods, either by excessive labors, persuading the soul that this is the way to find God, and thus choking the internal process of the interior life, or, by this tension of the mind, of which I have spoken. Neither of these methods open in the soul, the interior way.

You reply, how, then, is this life accomplished? I answer, God, seeing the heart of him who seeks him within, draws near to him, and teaches him a just moderation in all things; and, by this retrenchment of all excess in externals, the soul begins to perceive the peaceful kingdom. It realizes within itself a guide, who provides for its necessities, according to divine laws, who takes away the burdens that sin imposes; a guide who does not foster corrupt nature, nor forbid innocent pleasures.

When the soul begins to perceive this kingdom, and that the King himself is manifested in some degree, it thus communes, (and we may call this the second step), O, my Beloved, I have sought thee with all the strength of my heart, in the place where thou hast taught me to seek thee, and I have there found thee! Days and nights have I passed in seeking thee. All the desires of my heart go after thee. But now I have found thee. I pray thee to reign as Sovereign, to establish thine empire in my soul. I will do thy will alone. I will resign to thee all the right I have to myself; all that thou, by thy goodness, hast given to me.

At this stage of progress, the soul ceases from self. Its work is to regard, lovingly, the operation of God, without a desire either to advance it, or place any obstacle in the way of its progress. The soul has been active, in the first stage, to destroy, with all its power, that which might hinder the kingdom of God within; and this was a great effort; for habit had rendered interior recollection very difficult, and the powers of the soul did not easily reunite themselves in one center.

Now the soul seeks no longer to combat the obstacles, which hindered its return within, but lets God combat and act in the soul. Saying, it is time O, Lord, that thou shouldst take possession of thy kingdom! Do so, I pray thee, exclusively. I desire, on my part, only to observe thine operation.

This commencement of the reign of God, and of the passive way, is very highly relished by the soul. The soul passes days, and even years, separated from creature enjoyments without weariness. It advances very much more by this way, in little time, than by all the efforts of many years. It is not without faults and imperfections, but divine love diminishes them little by little, or does not permit the soul to become disturbed by them, lest it become discouraged and its love hindered. This state is called passive love. The soul sees no cause to fear; it supposes that all the work is done, and that it has only to pass into eternity, and to enjoy this good Sovereign, who already gives himself to the soul in so much fullness.

But in the onward progress of the soul, it becomes no longer doubtful, whether the soul is to remain in the passive enjoyment of God and his communications. The soul begins to feel a drawing, to let God not only be all things in the soul, but there to reign separate from the soul's enjoyment of his gifts. The soul now experiences what is called, by the author of the Imitation of Christ, the exile of the heart. It hears a voice in the depth of the soul, or, rather, has an impression, that God reigns there alone. This exile is at first very painful, for it is important to notice, that, from the commencement of seeking God in the depth of the soul to the possession of him, there are many trials, temptations, sorrows. Every successive state is marked by a purifying process. Persons often mistake, and take the first purification for the last. When God reigns alone in the soul, separate from the action of self, and self is destroyed, it is beyond any previous state.

When the soul has ceased from its own selfish operations, and the man of sin is exterminated, its defects become more apparent, because God wishes it to comprehend what it is by itself, and what it would be without him. The soul is thus afflicted, believing it has lost the virtues, acquired with so much care, and seems to have faults that it had not before perceived. It says, with the spouse in the Canticles, "I have washed my feet, how shall I sully them?" You do not perceive, O, soul beloved, that you do not sully them in going to "open to the spouse," and that if you contract some slight impurity, he will remove it so perfectly, that you will become more beautiful. In the mean time, it is not the desire of the spouse to become beautiful in her own eyes, but to see only the beauty of her Lover.

When the soul is faithful in this state, and really desires to die to itself, she is pleased only with the beauty of her Beloved, and says his beauty shall be my beauty. But it is necessary to advance beyond this, for, after being despoiled of her beauty, it would be a selfishness much greater to appropriate to herself, the beauty of her Beloved. His beauty must remain untarnished, unappropriated by her; she must leave him all, and remain in her nothing, for the nothing is her proper place. This is Perfect Love, which regards God alone.

SELECTIONS FROM HER POETRY

A LITTLE BIRD I AM

"A little bird I am,
Shut from the fields of air;
And in my cage I sit and sing
To Him who placed me there;
Well pleased a prisoner to be,
Because, my God, it pleases thee.

"Nought have I else to do;
I sing the whole day long;
And He, whom most I love to please,
Doth listen to my song;
He caught and bound my wandering wing,
But still he bends to hear me sing.

"Thou hast an ear to hear;
A heart to love and bless;
And, though my notes were e'er so rude,
Thou wouldst not hear the less;
Because though knowest as they fall,
That Love, sweet Love, inspires them all.

"My cage confines me round,
Abroad I cannot fly;
But, though my wing is closely bound,
My heart's at liberty.
My prison walls cannot control
The flight, the freedom of the soul.

"Oh! it is good to soar,
These bolts and bars above,
To Him whose purpose I adore,
Whose Providence I love;
And in thy mighty will to find
The joy, the freedom of the mind."

GOD EVERYWHERE, TO THE SOUL THAT LOVES HIM

"Oh! Thou by long experience tried,
Near whom no grief can long abide;
My Lord! how full of sweet content,
I pass my years of banishment.

"All scenes alike engaging prove,
To souls impressed with sacred love;
Where'er they dwell, they dwell in Thee,
In Heaven, in earth, or on the sea.

"To me remains nor place nor time,
My country is in every clime,
I can be calm and free from care
On any shore, since God is there.

"While place we seek, or place we shun,
The soul finds happiness in none;
But with a God to guide our way,
'Tis equal joy to go or stay.

"Could I be cast where Thou art not,
That were indeed a dreadful lot;
But regions none remote I call,
Secure of finding God in all.

"My country, Lord, art Thou alone;

No other can I claim or own;
The point where all my wishes meet,
My law, my love; life's only sweet.

"I love my God, but with no love of mine,
For I have none to give;
I love thee, Lord; but all the love is thine,
For by thy life I live.
I am as nothing, and rejoice to be
Emptied, and lost, and swallowed up in thee.

"Thou, Lord, alone, art all thy children need,
And there is none beside;
From thee the streams of blessedness proceed;
In thee the bless'd abide.
Fountain of life, and all-abounding grace,
Our source, our center, and our dwelling-place."

A Short Method of Prayer

Translated from the Paris Edition of 1790
by
A. W. MARSTON (1875)

PREFACE TO THE ENGLISH PROTESTANT EDITION

Some apology is perhaps needed when a Protestant thus brings before Protestant readers the works of a consistent Roman Catholic author. The plea must be, that the doctrine and experience described are essentially Protestant; and so far from their receiving the assent of the Roman Catholic Church, their author was persecuted for holding and disseminating them.

Of the experience of Madame Guyon, it should be borne in mind, that though the glorious heights of communion with God to which she attained may be scaled by the feeblest of God's chosen ones, yet it is by no means necessary that they should be reached by the same apparently arduous and protracted path along which she was led.

The "Torrents" especially needs to be regarded rather as an account of the personal experience of the author, than as the plan which God invariably, or even usually, adopts in bringing the soul into a state of union with Himself. It is true that, in order that we may "live unto righteousness," we must be "dead indeed unto sin;" and that there must be a crucifixion of self before the life of Christ can be made manifest in us. It is only when we can say, "I am crucified with Christ," that we are able to add, "Nevertheless I live, yet not I, but Christ liveth in me." But it does not follow that this inward death must always be as lingering as in the case of Madame Guyon. She tells us herself that the reason was, that she was not wholly resigned to the Divine will, and willing to be deprived of the gifts of God, that she might enjoy the possession of the Giver. This resistance to the will of God implies suffering on the part of the creature, and chastisement on the part of God, in order that He may subdue to Himself what is not voluntarily yielded to Him.

Of the joy of a complete surrender to God, it is not necessary to speak here: thousands of God's children are realizing its blessedness for themselves, and proving that it is no hardship, but a joy unspeakable, to present themselves a living sacrifice to God, to live no longer to themselves, but to Him that died for them, and rose again.

A simple trust in a living, personal Savior; a putting away by His grace of all that is known to be in opposition to His will; and an entire self-abandonment to Him, that His designs may be worked out in and through us; such is the simple key to the hidden sanctuary of communion.

"Walk before me, and be thou perfect." (Gen. 17:1)

AUTHOR'S PREFACE

I did not write this little work with the thought of its being given to the public. It was prepared for the help of a few Christians who were desirous of loving God with the whole heart. But so many have requested copies of it, because of the benefit they have derived from its perusal, that I have been asked to publish it.

I have left it in its natural simplicity. I do not condemn the opinions of any: on the contrary, I esteem those which are held by others, and submit all that I have written to the censure of persons of experience and learning. I only ask of all that they will not be content with examining the outside, but that they will penetrate the design of the writer, which is only to lead others to love God, and to serve Him with greater happiness and success, by enabling them to do it in a simple and easy way, fit for the little ones who are not capable of extraordinary things, but who truly desire to give themselves to God.

I ask all who may read it, to read without prejudice; and they will discover, under common expressions, a hidden unction, which will lead them to seek for a happiness which all ought to expect to possess.

I use the word facility, saying that perfection is easy, because it is easy to find God, when we seek Him within ourselves. The passage may be quoted which says, "Ye shall seek me, and shall not find me" (John 7:34). Yet this need not occasion any difficulty; because the same God, who cannot contradict Himself, has said, "He that seeketh findeth" (Matt. 7:8). He who seeks God, and who yet is unwilling to forsake sin, will not find Him, because he is seeking Him where He cannot be found; therefore it is added, "Ye shall die in your sins." But he who sincerely desires to forsake sin, that he may draw near to God, will find Him infallibly.

Many people imagine religion so frightful, and prayer so extraordinary, that they are not willing to strive after them, never expecting to attain to them. But as the difficulty which we see in a thing causes us to despair of succeeding in it, and at the same time removes the desire to undertake it; and as, when a thing appears both desirable and easy to be attained, we give ourselves to it with pleasure, and pursue it boldly; I have been constrained to set forth the advantage and the facility of this way.

Oh! if we were persuaded of the goodness of God toward His poor creatures, and of the desire which He has to communicate Himself to them, we should not imagine so many obstacles, and despair so easily of obtaining a good which He is so infinitely desirous of imparting to us.

And if He has not spared His own Son, but delivered Him up for us all, is there anything He can refuse us? Assuredly not. We only need a little courage and perseverance. We have so much of both for trifling temporal interests, and we have none for the "one thing needful."

As for those who find a difficulty in believing that it is easy to find God in this way, let them not believe all that they are told, but rather let them make trial of it, that they may judge for themselves; and they will find that I say very little in comparison with that which is.

Dear reader, study this little work with a simple and sincere heart, with lowliness of mind, without wishing to criticize it, and you will find it of good to you. Receive it with the same spirit as that in which it is given, which is no other than the longing that you may be led to give yourself unreservedly to God. My desire is that it may be the means of leading the simple ones and the children to their Father, who loves their humble confidence, and to whom distrust is so displeasing. Seek nothing but the love of God; have a sincere desire for your salvation, and you will assuredly find it, following this little unmethodical method.

I do not pretend to elevate my sentiments above those of others, but I relate simply what has been my own experience as well as that of others, and the advantage which I have found in this simple and natural manner of going to God.

If this book treats of nothing else but the short and easy method of prayer, it is because, being written only for that, it cannot speak of other things. It is certain that, if it be read in the spirit in which it has been written, there will be found nothing in it to shock the mind. Those who will make the experience of it will be the most certain of the truth which it contains.

It is to Thee, O Holy Child Jesus, who lovest simplicity and innocence, and who findest Thy delight in the children of men, that is to say, with those among men who are willing to become children;—it is to Thee, I say, to give worth and value to this little work, impressing it on the heart, and leading those who read it to seek Thee within themselves, where Thou wilt take Thy rest, receiving the tokens of their love, and giving them proofs of Thine.

It is Thy work, O Divine Child! O uncreated Love! O silent Word! to make Thyself beloved, tasted, and heard. Thou art able to do it; and I even dare to say that Thou wilt do it, by means of this little work, which is all to Thee, all of Thee, and all for Thee.

Chapter 1

ALL ARE COMMANDED TO PRAY

PRAYER THE GREAT MEANS OF SALVATION, AND POSSIBLE AT ALL TIMES BY THE MOST SIMPLE

PRAYER is nothing else but the application of the heart to God, and the interior exercise of love. St Paul commands us to "pray without ceasing" (1 Thess. 5:17). Our Lord says: "Take ye heed, watch and pray." "And what I say unto you, I say unto all" (Mark 13:33, 37). All, then, are capable of prayer, and it is the duty of all to engage in it.

But I do not think that all are fit for 2meditation; and, therefore, it is not that sort of prayer which God demands or desires of them.

My dear friends, whoever you may be, who desire to be saved, come unto God in prayer. "I counsel thee to buy of me gold tried in the fire, that thou mayest be rich" (Rev. 3:18). It is easily to be obtained, far more easily than you could ever imagine.

Come, all ye that are athirst, and take this water of life freely (see Rev. 22:17). Do not amuse yourselves by hewing out to yourselves "broken cisterns that can hold no water" (Jer. 2:13). Come, hungry souls, who find nothing that can satisfy you, and you shall be filled. Come, poor afflicted ones, weighed down with griefs and sorrows, and you shall be comforted. Come, sick ones, to the great Physician, and do not fear to approach Him because you are so weak and diseased: expose all your diseases to Him, and they shall be healed.

Come, children, to your Father; He will receive you with open arms of love. Come, wandering and scattered sheep, to your Shepherd. Come, sinners, to your Savior. Come, ignorant and foolish ones, who believe yourselves incapable of prayer; it is you who are the most fitted for it. Come all without exception; Jesus Christ calls you all.

Let those only refuse to come who have no heart. The invitation is not for them; for we must have a heart in order to love. But who is indeed without heart? Oh, come and give that heart to God, and learn in the place of prayer how to do it! All those who long for prayer are capable of it, who have ordinary grace and the gift of the Holy Spirit, which is freely promised to all who ask it.

Prayer is the key of perfection and of sovereign happiness; it is the efficacious means of getting rid of all vices and of acquiring all virtues; for the way to become perfect is to live in the presence of God. He tells us this Himself: "Walk before me, and be thou perfect" (Gen. 17:1). Prayer alone can bring you into His presence, and keep you there continually.

What we need, then, is an attitude of prayer, in which we can constantly abide, and out of which exterior occupations cannot draw us; a prayer which can be offered alike by princes, kings, prelates, magistrates, soldiers, children, artisans, laborers, women, and the sick. This prayer is not mental, but of the heart.

It is not a prayer of thought alone, because the mind of man is so limited, that while it is occupied with one thing it cannot be thinking of another. But it is the prayer of the heart, which cannot be interrupted by the occupations of the mind. Nothing can interrupt the prayer of the heart but unruly affections; and when once we have tasted of the love of God, it is impossible to find our delight in anything but Himself.

Nothing is easier than to have God and to live upon Him. He is more truly in us than we are in ourselves. He is more anxious to give Himself to us than we are to possess Him. All that we want is to know the way to seek Him, which is so easy and so natural, that breathing itself is not more so.

Oh, you who imagine yourselves incapable of religious feeling, you may live in prayer and in 5God as easily and as continuously as you live by the air you breathe. Will you not, then, be inexcusable if you neglect to do it, after you have learned the way?

Chapter 2

FIRST DEGREE OF PRAYER

MEDITATION AND MEDITATIVE READING — THE LORD'S PRAYER — PASSAGE FROM THE FIRST DEGREE TO THE SECOND

THERE are two means by which we may be led into the higher forms of prayer. One is Meditation, the other is Meditative Reading. By meditative reading I mean the taking of some truths, either doctrinal or practical—the latter rather than the former—and reading them in this way:—Take the truth which has presented itself to you, and read two or three lines, seeking to enter into the full meaning of the words, and go on no further so long as you find satisfaction in them; leave the place only when it becomes insipid. After that, take another passage, and do the same, not reading more than half a page at once.

It is not so much from the amount read that we derive profit, as from the manner of reading. Those people who get through so much do not profit from it; the bees can only draw the juice from the flowers by resting on them, not by flying round them. Much reading is more for scholastic than for spiritual science; but in order to derive profit from spiritual books, we should read them in this way; and I am sure that this manner of reading accustoms us gradually to prayer, and gives us a deeper desire for it. The other way is Meditation, in which we should engage at a chosen time, and not in the hour given to reading. I think the way to enter into it is this:—After having brought ourselves into the presence of God by a definite act of faith, we should read something substantial, not so much to reason upon it, as to fix the attention, observing that the principal exercise should be the presence of God, and that the subject should rather fix the attention than exercise reason.

This faith in the presence of God within our hearts must lead us to enter within ourselves, collecting our thoughts, and preventing their wandering; this is an effectual way of getting rid of distracting thoughts, and of losing sight of outward things, in order to draw near to God, who can only be found in the secret place of our hearts, which is the sancta-sanctorum in which He dwells.

He has promised that if any one keeps His commandments, He will come to him, and make His abode with him (John 14:23). St Augustine reproaches himself for the time he lost through not having sought God at first in this way.

When, then, we are thus buried in ourselves, and deeply penetrated with the presence of God within us—when the senses are all drawn from the circumference to the center, which, though it is not easily accomplished at first, becomes quite natural afterwards—when the soul is thus gathered up within itself, and is sweetly occupied with the truth read, not in reasoning upon it, but in feeding upon it, and exciting the will by the affection rather than the understanding by consideration: the affection being thus touched, must be suffered to repose sweetly and at peace, swallowing what it has tasted.

As a person who only masticated an excellent meat would not be nourished by it, although he would be sensible of its taste, unless he ceased this movement in order to swallow it; so when the affection is stirred, if we seek continually to stir it, we extinguish its fire, and thus deprive the soul of its nourishment. We must swallow by a loving repose (full of respect and confidence) what we have masticated and tasted. This method is very necessary, and would advance the soul in a short time more than any other would do in several years.

But as I said that the direct and principal exercise should be the sense of the presence of God, we must most faithfully recall the senses when they wander.

This is a short and efficacious way of fighting with distractions; because those who endeavor directly to oppose them, irritate and increase them; but by losing ourselves in the thought of a present God, and suffering our thoughts to be drawn to Him, we combat them indirectly, and without thinking of them, but in an effectual manner. And here let me warn beginners not to run from one truth to another, from one subject to another; but to keep themselves to one so long as they feel a taste for it: this is the way to enter deeply into truths, to taste them, and to have them impressed upon us. I say it is difficult at first thus to retire within ourselves, because of the habits, which are natural to us, of being taken up with the outside; but when we are a little accustomed to it, it becomes exceedingly easy; both because we have formed the habit of it, and because God, who only desires to communicate Himself to us, sends us abundant grace, and an experimental sense of His presence, which renders it easy.

Let us apply this method to the Lord's Prayer. We say "Our Father," thinking that God is within us, and will indeed be our Father. After having pronounced this word Father, we remain a few moments in silence, waiting for this heavenly Father to make known His will to us. Then we ask this King of Glory to reign within us, abandoning ourselves to Him, that He may do it, and yielding to Him the right that He has over us. If we feel here an inclination to peace and silence, we should not continue, but remain thus so long as the condition may last; after which we proceed to the second petition, "Thy will be done on earth, as it is in heaven." We then desire that God may accomplish, in us and by us, all His will; we give up to God our heart and our liberty, that He may dispose of them at His pleasure. Then, seeing that the occupation of the will should be love, we desire to love, and we ask God to give us His love. But all this is done quietly, peacefully; and so on with the rest of the prayer.

At other times we hold ourselves in the position of sheep near to the Shepherd, asking of Him our true food. O Divine Shepherd! Thou feedest Thy sheep with Thine own hand, and Thou art their food from day to day. We may also bring before Him our family desires; but it must all be done with the remembrance by faith of the presence of God within us.

We can form no imagination of what God is: a lively faith in His presence is sufficient; for we can conceive no image of God, though we may of Christ, regarding Him as crucified, or as a child, or in some other condition, provided that we always seek Him within ourselves.

At other times we come to Him as to a Physician, bringing our maladies to Him that He may heal them; but always without effort, with a short silence from time to time, that the silence may be mingled with the action, gradually lengthening the silence and shortening the spoken prayer, until at length, as we yield to the operation of God, He gains the supremacy. When the presence of God is given, and the soul begins to taste of silence and repose, this experimental sense of the presence of God introduces it to the second degree of prayer.

Chapter 3

SECOND DEGREE OF PRAYER

CALLED HERE "THE PRAYER OF SIMPLICITY."

THE second degree has been variously termed Contemplation, The Prayer of Silence, and of repose; while others again have called it the Prayer of Simplicity; and it is of this last term that I shall make use here, being more appropriate than that of Contemplation, which signifies a degree of prayer more advanced than that of which I speak.

After a time, as I have said, the soul becomes sensible of a facility in recognizing the presence of God; it collects itself more easily; prayer becomes natural and pleasant; it knows that it leads to God; and it perceives the smell of His perfumes.

Then it must change its method, and observe carefully what I am about to say, without being astonished at its apparent implausibility.

First of all, when you bring yourself into the presence of God by faith, remain a short time in an attitude of respectful silence. If from the beginning, in making this act of faith, you are sensible of a little taste of the presence of God, remain as you are without troubling yourself on any subject, and keep that which has been given you, so long as it may remain.

If it leaves you, excite your will by means of some tender affection, and if you then find that your former state of peace has returned, remain in it. The fire must be blown softly, and as soon as it is lighted, cease to blow it, or you will put it out. It is also necessary that you should go to God, not so much to obtain something from Him, as to please Him, and to do His will; for a servant who only serves his master in proportion to the recompense he receives, is unworthy of any remuneration.

Go, then, to prayer, not only to enjoy God, but to be as He wills: this will keep you equal in times of barrenness and in times of abundance; and you will not be dismayed by the repulses of God, nor by His apparent indifference.

Chapter 4

ON SPIRITUAL DRYNESS

AS God's only desire is to give Himself to the loving soul who desires to seek Him, He often hides Himself in order to arouse it, and compel it to seek Him with love and fidelity. But how does He reward the faithfulness of His beloved! And how are His apparent flights followed by loving caresses!

The soul imagines that it is a proof of its fidelity and of its increased love that it seeks God with an effort, or that at least such seeking will soon lead to His return.

But no! This is not the way in this degree. With a loving impatience, with deep humility and abasement, with an affection deep and yet restful, with a respectful silence, you must await the return of your Beloved.

You will thus show Him that it is Himself alone that you love, and His good pleasure, and not the pleasure that you find in loving Him. Therefore it is said, "Make not haste in time of trouble. Cleave unto Him, and depart not away, that thou mayest be increased at thy last end" (Ecclus. 2:2, 3). Suffer the suspensions and the delays of the visible consolations of God.

Be patient in prayer, even though you should do nothing all your life but wait in patience, with a heart humbled, abandoned, resigned, and content for the return of your Beloved. Oh, excellent prayer! How it moves the heart of God, and obliges Him to return more than anything else!

Chapter 5

ABANDONMENT TO GOD

ITS FRUIT AND ITS IRREVOCABILITY — IN WHAT IT CONSISTS — GOD EXHORTS US TO IT.

IT is here that true abandonment and consecration to God should commence, by our being deeply convinced that all which happens to us moment by moment is the will of God, and therefore all that is necessary to us.

This conviction will render us contented with everything, and will make us see the commonest events in God, and not in the creature.

I beg of you, whoever you may be, who are desirous of giving yourselves to God, not to take yourselves back when once you are given to Him, and to remember that a thing once given away is no longer at your disposal. Abandonment is the key to the inner life: he who is thoroughly abandoned will soon be perfect.

You must, then, hold firmly to your abandonment, without listening to reason or to reflection. A great faith makes a great abandonment; you must trust wholly in God, against hope believing in hope (Rom. 4:18). Abandonment is the casting off of all care of ourselves, to leave ourselves to be guided entirely by God.

All Christians are exhorted to abandonment, for it is said to all, "Take no thought for the morrow; for your Heavenly Father knoweth that ye have need of all these things" (Matt. 6:32,

34). "In all thy ways acknowledge Him, and He shall direct thy paths" (Prov. 3:6). "Commit thy works unto the Lord, and thy thoughts shall be established" (Prov. 16:3). "Commit thy way unto the Lord; trust also in Him; and He shall bring it to pass" (Ps. 37:5).

Abandonment, then, ought to be an utter leaving of ourselves, both outwardly and inwardly, in the hands of God, forgetting ourselves, and thinking only of God. By this means the heart is kept always free and contented.

Practically it should be a continual loss of our own will in the will of God, a renunciation of all natural inclinations, however good they may appear, in order that we may be left free to choose only as God chooses: we should be indifferent to all things, whether temporal or spiritual, for the body or the soul; leaving the past in forgetfulness, the future to providence, and giving the present to God; contented with the present moment, which brings with it God's eternal will for us; attributing nothing which happens to us to the creature, but seeing all things in God, and regarding them as coming infallibly from His hand, with the exception only of our own sin.

Leave yourselves, then, to be guided by God as He will, whether as regards the inner or the outward life.

Chapter 6

OF SUFFERING WHICH MUST BE ACCEPTED

AS FROM GOD--ITS FRUITS

BE content with all the suffering that God may lay upon you. If you will love Him purely, you will be as willing to follow Him to Calvary as to Tabor.

He must be loved as much on Calvary as on Tabor, since it is there that He makes the greatest manifestation of His love.

Do not act, then, like those people who give themselves at one time, and take themselves back at another. They give themselves to be caressed, and take themselves back when they are crucified; or else they seek for consolation in the creature.

You can only find consolation in the love of the cross and in complete abandonment. He who has no love for the cross has no love for God (see Matt. 16:24). It is impossible to love God without loving the cross; and a heart which has learned to love the cross finds sweetness, joy, and pleasure even in the bitterest things. "To the hungry soul every bitter thing is sweet" (Prov. 27:7), because it is as hungry for the cross as it is hungry for God.

The cross gives God, and God gives the cross. Abandonment and the cross go together. As soon as you are sensible that something is repugnant to you which presents itself to you in the light of suffering, abandon yourself at once to God for that very thing, and present yourself as a sacrifice to Him: you will see that, when the cross comes, it will have lost much of its weight, because you will desire it. This will not prevent your being sensible of its weight. Some people imagine that it is not suffering to feel the cross. The feeling of suffering is one of the principal parts of suffering itself. Jesus Himself was willing to suffer it in its intensity.

Often the cross is borne with weakness, at other times with strength: all should be equal in the will of God.

Chapter 7

ON MYSTERIES

GOD GIVES THEM HERE IN REALITY

IT will be objected that, by this way, mysteries will not be made known. It is just the contrary; they are given to the soul in reality. Jesus Christ, to whom it is abandoned, and whom it follows as the Way, whom it hears as the Truth, and who animates it as the Life, impressing Himself upon it, imparts to it His own condition.

To bear the conditions of Christ is something far greater than merely to consider those conditions. Paul bore the conditions of Christ on his body. "I bear in my body," he says, "the marks of the Lord Jesus" (Gal. 6:17). But he does not say that he reasoned about them.

Often Christ gives in this state of abandonment views of His conditions in a striking manner. We must receive equally all the dispositions in which He may be pleased to place us, choosing for ourselves to abide near to Him, and to be annihilated before Him, but receiving equally all that He gives us, light or darkness, facility or barrenness, strength or weakness, sweetness or bitterness, temptations or distractions, sorrow, care, uncertainty; none of these things ought to move us.

There are some persons to whom God is continually revealing His mysteries: let them be faithful to them. But when God sees fit to remove them, let them suffer them to be taken.

Others are troubled because no mysteries are made known to them: this is needless, since a loving attention to God includes all particular devotion, and that which is united to God alone, by its rest in Him, is instructed in a most excellent manner in all mysteries. He who loves God loves all that is of Him.

Chapter 8

ON VIRTUE

ALL VIRTUES GIVEN WITH GOD IN THIS DEGREE
OF THE PRAYER OF THE HEART

THIS is the short and the sure way of acquiring virtue; because, God being the principle of all virtue, we possess all virtue in possessing God.

More than this, I say that all virtue which is not given inwardly is a mask of virtue, and like a garment that can be taken off, and will wear out. But virtue communicated fundamentally is essential, true, and permanent. "The King's daughter is all glorious within" (Ps. 45:13). And there are none who practise virtue more constantly than those who acquire it in this way, though virtue is not a distinct subject of their thought.

How hungry these loving ones are after suffering! They think only of what can please their Beloved, and they begin to neglect themselves, and to think less of themselves. The more they love God, the more they hate themselves.

Oh, if all could learn this method, so easy that it is suited for all, for the most ignorant as for the most learned, how easily the whole Church would be reformed! You only need to love. St Augustine says, "Love, and do as you please;" for when we love perfectly, we shall not desire to do anything that could be displeasing to our Beloved.

Chapter 9

OF PERFECT CONVERSION

WHICH IS AN EFFECT OF THIS METHOD OF PRAYER—TWO OF ITS AIDS, THE ATTRACTION OF GOD, AND THE CENTRAL INCLINATION OF THE SOUL

"TURN ye unto Him from whom the children of Israel have deeply revolted" (Isa. 31:6). Conversion is nothing else but a turning from the creature to God. Conversion is not perfect, though it is necessary for salvation, when it is merely a turning from sin to grace. To be complete, it must be a turning from without to within.

The soul, being turned in the direction of God, has a great facility for remaining converted to Him. The longer it is converted, the nearer it approaches to God, and attaches itself to Him; and the nearer it approaches to God, the more it becomes necessarily drawn from the creature, which is opposed to God.

But this cannot be done by a violent effort of the creature; all that it can do is to remain turned in the direction of God in a perpetual adherence.

God has an attracting virtue, which draws the soul more strongly towards Himself; and in attracting it, He purifies it: as we see the sun attracting a dense vapor, and gradually, without any other effort on the part of the vapor than that of letting itself be drawn, the sun, by bringing it near to himself, refines and purifies it.

There is, however, this difference, that the vapor is not drawn freely, and does not follow willingly, as is the case with the soul.

This manner of turning within is very simple, and makes the soul advance naturally and without effort; because God is its center. The center has always a strong attractive power; and the larger the center, the stronger is its attractive force.

Besides this attraction of the center, there is given to all natural objects a strong tendency to become united with their center. As soon as anything is turned in the direction of its center, unless it be stopped by some invincible obstacle, it rushes towards it with extreme velocity. A stone in the air is no sooner let loose, and turned towards the earth, than it tends to it by its own weight as its center. It is the same with fire and water, which, being no longer arrested, run incessantly towards their center.

Now I say that the soul, by the effort it has made in inward recollection, being turned towards its center, without any other effort, but simply by the weight of love, falls towards its center; and the more it remains quiet and at rest, making no movement of its own, the more rapidly it will advance, because it thus allows that attractive virtue to draw it.

All the care, then, that we need have is to promote this inward recollection as much as possible, not being astonished at the difficulty we may find in this exercise, which will soon be recompensed with a wonderful co-operation on the part of God, which will render it very easy. When the passions rise, a look towards God, who is present within us, easily deadens them. Any other resistance would irritate rather than appease them.

Chapter 10

HIGHER DEGREE OF PRAYER

WHICH IS THAT OF THE SIMPLE PRESENCE OF GOD, OR ACTIVE CONTEMPLATION

THE soul, faithfully exercising itself in the affection and

love of its God, is astonished to find Him taking complete possession of it.

His presence becomes so natural, that it would be impossible not to have it: it becomes habitual to the soul, which is also conscious of a great calm spreading over it. Its prayer is all silence, and God imparts to it an intrinsic love, which is the commencement of ineffable happiness.

Oh, if I could describe the infinite degrees which follow! But I must stop here, since I am writing for beginners, and wait till God shall bring to light what may be useful to those more advanced.1 I can only say, that, at this point, it is most important that all natural operation should cease, that God may act alone: "Be still, and know that I am God," is His own word by David (Ps. 46:10).

But man is so attached to his own works, that he cannot believe God is working, unless he can feel, know, and distinguish His operation. He does not see that it is the speed of his course which prevents his seeing the extent of his advancement; and that the operation of God becoming more abundant, absorbs that of the creature, as we see that the sun, in proportion as he rises, absorbs the light of the stars, which were easily distinguishable before he appeared. It is not the want of light, but an excess of light, which prevents our distinguishing the stars.

It is the same here; man can no longer distinguish his own operation, because the strong light absorbs all his little distinct lights, and makes them fade away entirely, because God's excess surpasses them all. So that those who accuse this degree of prayer of being a state of idleness, are greatly deceived; and only speak thus from want of experience. Oh, if they would only prove it! in how short a time they would become experimentally acquainted with this matter!

I say, then, that this failure of work does not spring from scarcity, but from abundance.

Two classes of persons are silent: the one because they have nothing to say, the other because they have too much. It is thus in this degree. We are silent from excess, not from want.

Water causes death to two persons in very different ways. One dies of thirst, another is drowned: the one dies from want, the other from abundance. So here it is abundance which causes the cessation of natural operation. It is therefore important in this degree to remain as much as possible in stillness.

At the commencement of this prayer, a movement of affection is necessary; but when grace begins to flow into us, we have nothing to do but to remain at rest, and take all that God gives. Any other movement would prevent our profiting by this grace, which is given in order to draw us into the rest of love.

The soul in this peaceful attitude of prayer falls into a mystic sleep, in which all its natural powers are silenced, until that which had been temporary becomes its permanent condition. You see that the soul is thus led, without effort, without study, without artifice.

The heart is not a fortified place, which must be taken by cannonading and violence: it is a kingdom of peace, which is possessed by love. Gently following in His train, you will soon reach the degree of intuitive prayer. God asks nothing extraordinary and difficult: on the contrary, He is most pleased with childlike simplicity.

The grandest part of religion is the most simple. It is the same with natural things. Do you wish to get to the sea? Embark upon a river, and insensibly and without effort you will be taken to it. Do you wish to get to God? Take His way, so quiet, so easy, and in a little while you will be taken to Him in a manner that will surprise you. Oh, if only you would try it! How soon you would see that I am telling you only too little, and that the experience would far surpass any description that could be given! What do you fear? Why do you not throw yourself at once into the arms of Love, who only stretched them out upon the cross in order to take you in? What risk can there be in trusting God, and abandoning yourself to Him? Oh, He will not deceive you, unless it be by giving you far more than you ever expected: while those who expect everything from themselves may well take to themselves the reproach which God utters by the mouth of Isaiah: "Thou art wearied in the greatness of thy way; yet saidst thou not, There is no hope" (Isa. 62:10).

Chapter 11

OF REST IN THE PRESENCE OF GOD

INWARD AND OUTWARD SILENCE, ITS FRUITS — INWARD SILENCE — GOD COMMANDS IT — OUTWARD SILENCE

THE soul, being brought to this place, needs no other preparation than that of repose: for the presence of God during the day, which is the great result of prayer, or rather prayer itself, begins to be intuitive and almost continual. The soul is conscious of a deep inward happiness, and feels that God is in it more truly than it is in itself. It has only one thing to do in order to find God, which is to retire within itself. As soon as the eyes are closed, it finds itself in prayer.

It is astonished at this infinite happiness; there is carried on within it a conversation which outward things cannot interrupt. It might be said of this method of prayer, as was said of Wisdom, "All good things together come to me with her" (Wisdom of Solomon 7:11), for virtue flows naturally into the soul, and is practised so easily, that it seems to be quite natural to it. It has within it a germ of life and fruitfulness, which gives it a facility for all good, and an insensibility to all evil. Let it then remain faithful, and seek no other frame of mind than that of simple rest. It has only to suffer itself to be filled with this divine effusion.

"The Lord is in His holy temple: let all the earth keep silence before Him" (Hab. 2:20). The reason why inward silence is so necessary is, that Christ, being the eternal and essential Word, in order that He may be received into the soul, there must be a disposition corresponding with what He is. Now it is certain that in order to receive words we must listen. Hearing is the sense given to enable us to receive the words which are communicated to us. Hearing is rather a passive than an active sense, receiving, and not communicating. Christ being the Word which is to be communicated, the soul must be attentive to this Word which speaks within it.

This is why we are so often exhorted to listen to God, and to be attentive to His voice. Many passages might be quoted. I will be content to mention a few: "Hearken unto me, O my people; and give ear unto me, O my nation" (Isa. 51:4). "Hearken unto me, O house of Jacob, and all the remnant of the house of Israel" (Isa. 46:31). "Hearken, O daughter, and consider, and incline thine ear; forget also thine own people, and thy father's house; so shall the King greatly desire thy beauty" (Ps. 45:10, 11).

We must listen to God, and be attentive to Him, forgetting ourselves and all self-interest. These two actions, or rather passions—for this condition is essentially a passive one—arouse in God a "desire" towards the "beauty" He has Himself communicated.

Outward silence is extremely necessary for the cultivation of inward silence, and it is impossible to acquire inward silence without having a love for silence and solitude.

God tells us by the mouth of His prophet, "I will allure her, and bring her into the wilderness, and speak to her heart" (marginal reading of Hosea 2:14).

To be inwardly occupied with God, and outwardly occupied with countless trifles, this is impossible.

It will be a small matter to pray, and to retire within ourselves for half an hour or an hour, if we do not retain the unction and the spirit of prayer during the day.

Chapter 12

SELF-EXAMINATION AND CONFESSION

SELF-EXAMINATION should always precede confession. Those who arrive at this degree should expose themselves to God, who will not fail to enlighten them, and to make known to them the nature of their faults. This examination must be conducted in peace and tranquility, expecting more from God than from our own research the knowledge of our sins.

When we examine ourselves with an effort, we easily make mistakes. We "call evil good, and good evil;" and self-esteem easily deceives us. But when we remain exposed to the searching gaze of God, that Divine Sun brings to light even the smallest atoms. We must then, for self-examination, abandon ourselves utterly to God.

When we are in this degree of prayer, God is not slow to reveal to us all the faults we commit. We have no sooner sinned than we feel a burning reproach.

It is God Himself who conducts an examination which

nothing escapes, and we have only to turn towards God, and suffer the pain and the correction which He gives. As this examination by God is continual, we can no longer examine ourselves; and if we are faithful to our abandonment to God, we shall soon be better examined by the divine light than we could be by all our own efforts. Experience will make this known. One thing which often causes astonishment to the soul is, that when it is conscious of a sin, and comes to confess it to God, instead of feeling regret and contrition, such as it formerly felt, a sweet and gentle love takes possession of it.

Not having experienced this before, it supposes that it ought to draw itself out of this condition to make a definite act of contrition. But it does not see that, by doing this, it would lose true contrition, which is this intuitive love, infinitely greater than anything it could create for itself. It is a higher action, which includes the others, with greater perfection, though these are not possessed distinctly.

We should not seek to do anything for ourselves when God acts more excellently in us and for us. It is hating sin as God hates it to hate it in this way. This love, which is the operation of God in the soul, is the purest of all love. All we have to do then is to remain as we are.

Another remarkable thing is, that we often forget our faults, and find it difficult to remember them; but this must not trouble us, for two reasons: The first, that this very forgetfulness is a proof that the sin has been atoned for, and it is better to forget all that concerns ourselves, that we may remember God alone. The second reason is, that God does not fail, whenever confession is needful, to show to the soul its greatest faults, for then it is He Himself who examines it.

Chapter 13

ON READING — VOCAL PRAYER —EQUESTS

THE proper manner of reading in this degree is, as soon as we feel attracted to meditation, to cease reading, and remain at rest.

The soul is no sooner called to inward silence, than it should cease to utter vocal prayers; saying but little at any time, and when it does say them, if it finds any difficulty, or feels itself drawn to silence, it should remain silent, and make no effort to pray, leaving itself to the guidance of the Spirit of God.

The soul will find that it cannot, as formerly, present definite requests to God. This need not surprise it, for it is now that "the Spirit maketh intercession for the saints, according to the will of God. The Spirit also helpeth our infirmities: for we know not what we should pray for as we ought; but the Spirit itself maketh intercession for us, with groanings which cannot be uttered" (Rom. 8:26, 27).

We must second the designs of God, which are to strip the soul of its own works, to substitute His in their place.

Let Him work then, and bind yourself to nothing of your own. However good it may appear to you, it cannot be so if it comes in the way of God's will for you. The will of God is preferable to all other good. Seek not your own interests, but live by abandonment and by faith.

It is here that faith begins to operate wonderfully in the soul.

Chapter 14

THE FAULTS COMMITTED IN THIS DEGREE

DISTRACTIONS, TEMPTATIONS — THE COURSE TO BE PURSUED RESPECTING THEM

AS soon as we fall into a fault, or have wandered, we must turn again within ourselves; because this fault having turned us from God, we should as soon as possible turn towards Him, and suffer the penitence which He Himself will give.

It is of great importance that we should not be anxious about these faults, because the anxiety only springs from a secret pride and a love of our own excellence. We are troubled at feeling what we are.

If we become discouraged, we shall grow weaker yet; and reflection upon our faults produces a vexation which is worse than the sin itself.

A truly humble soul does not marvel at its weakness, and the more it perceives its wretchedness, the more it abandons itself to God, and seeks to remain near to Him, knowing how deeply it needs His help. God's own word to us is, "I will instruct thee, and teach thee in the way which thou shalt go: I will guide thee with mine eye" (Ps. 32:8).

In distractions or temptations, instead of combating them directly, which would only serve to augment them, and to wean us from God, with whom alone we ought to be occupied, we should simply turn away from them, and draw nearer to God; as a little child, seeing a fierce animal approaching it, would not stay to fight it, nor even to look at it, but would run for shelter to its mother's arms, where it would be safe. "God is in the midst of her, she shall not be moved: God shall help her, and that right early" (Ps. 46:5).

If we adopt any other course of action, if we attempt to attack our enemies in our weakness, we shall be wounded, even if we are not entirely defeated; but remaining in the simple presence of God, we find ourselves immediately fortified.

This was what David did: he says, "I have set the Lord always before me; because He is at my right hand, I shall not be moved. Therefore my heart is glad, and my glory rejoiceth; my flesh also shall rest in hope." It is also said by Moses, "The Lord shall fight for you, and ye shall hold your peace" (Exod. 14:14).

Chapter 15

PRAYER AND SACRIFICE EXPLAINED

BY THE SIMILITUDE OF A PERFUME — OUR ANNIHILATION IN THIS SACRIFICE — SOLIDITY AND FRUITFULNESS OF THIS PRAYER AS SET FORTH IN THE GOSPEL

PRAYER ought to be both petition and sacrifice.

Prayer, according to the testimony of St John, is an incense, whose perfume rises to God. Therefore it is said in the Revelation (chap. 8:3), that an angel held a censer, which contained the incense of the prayers of saints.

Prayer is an outpouring of the heart in the presence of God. "I have poured out my soul before the Lord," said the mother of Samuel (1 Sam.1:15). Thus the prayers of the Magi at the feet of the infant Jesus in the stable of Bethlehem were signified by the incense which they offered.

Prayer is the heat of love, which melts and dissolves the soul, and carries it to God. In proportion as it melts, it gives out its odor, and this odor comes from the love which burns it.

This is what the Bride meant when she said, "While the King sitteth at His table, my spikenard sendeth forth the smell thereof" (Cant. 1:12). The table is the heart. When God is there, and we are kept near to Him, in His presence, this presence of God melts and dissolves the hardness of our hearts, and as they melt, they give forth their perfume. Therefore the Bridegroom, seeing His Bride thus melted by the speech of her Beloved, says, "Who is this that cometh out of the wilderness, perfumed with myrrh and frankincense?" (Cant. 3:6).

Thus the soul rises up towards its God. But in order to this, it must suffer itself to be destroyed and annihilated by the force of love. This is a state of sacrifice essential to the Christian religion, by which the soul suffers itself to be destroyed and annihilated to render homage to the sovereignty of God; as it is written, "The power of the Lord is great, and He is honored of the lowly" (Ecclus. 3:20). And the destruction of our own being confesses the sovereign being of God.

We must cease to be, so that the Spirit of the Word may be in us. In order that He may come to us, we must yield our life to Him, and die to self that He may live in us, and that we being dead, our life may be hidden with Christ in God (Col. 3:3).

"Come unto me," says God, "all ye that be desirous of me, and fill yourselves with my fruits" (Ecclus. 24:19). But how can we be filled with God? Only by being emptied of self, and going out of ourselves in order to be lost in Him.

Now, this can never be brought about except by our becoming nothing. Nothingness is true prayer, which renders to God "honour, and glory, and power, for ever and ever" (Rev. v. 13).

This prayer is the prayer of truth. It is worshipping the Father in spirit and in truth. In spirit, because we are by it drawn out of our human and carnal action, to enter into the purity of the Spirit, who prays in us; and in truth, because the soul is led into the truth of the all of God, and the nothing of the creature.

There are but these two truths, the all and the nothing. All the rest is untruth.

We can only honor the all of God by our nothingness; and we have no sooner become nothing, than God, who will not suffer us to be empty, fills us with Himself. Oh, if all knew the blessings which come to the soul by this prayer, they would be satisfied with no others: it is the pearl of great price; it is the hidden treasure. He who finds it gladly sells all that he has to buy it (Matt. 13:44, 46). It is the well of living water, which springs up into everlasting life (John 4:14). It is the practice of the pure maxims of the gospel.

Does not Christ Himself tell us that the kingdom of God is within us? (Luke 17:21). This kingdom is set up in two ways. The first is, when God is so thoroughly master of us that nothing resists Him: then our heart is truly His kingdom. The other way is, that by possessing God, who is the sovereign Lord, we possess the kingdom of God, which is the height of felicity, and the end for which we were created. As it has been said, to serve God is to reign.

The end for which we were created is to enjoy God in this life, and men do not believe it!

Chapter 16

THIS STATE OF PRAYER NOT ONE OF IDLENESS

BUT OF NOBLE ACTION, WORKED BY THE SPIRIT OF GOD, AND IN DEPENDENCE UPON HIM—THE COMMUNICATION OF HIS LIFE AND UNION

SOME people, hearing of the prayer of silence, have wrongly imagined that the soul remains inactive, lifeless, and without movement.

But the truth is, that its action is more noble and more extensive than it ever was before it entered this degree, since it is moved by God Himself, and acted upon by His Spirit. St Paul desires that we should be led by the Spirit of God (Rom. 8:14). I do not say that there must be no action, but that we must act in dependence upon the divine movement. This is admirably set forth by Ezekiel. The prophet saw wheels which had the spirit of life, and wherever this spirit was to go, they went; they went on, or stood, or were lifted up, as they were moved, for the spirit of life was in them: but they never went back (see Ezek. 1:19–21). It should be the same with the soul: it should suffer itself to be moved and guided by the living Spirit who is in it, following His direction, and no other. Now this Spirit will never lead it to go backwards, that is, to reflect upon the creature, or to lean upon itself, but always to go forward, pressing continually towards the mark.

This action of the soul is a restful action. When it acts of itself, it acts with effort; and is therefore more conscious of its action. But when it acts in dependence upon the Spirit of grace, its action is so free, so easy, so natural, that it does not seem to act at all. "He brought me forth also into a large place; He delivered me, because He delighted in me" (Ps. 18:19).

As soon as the soul has commenced its course towards its center, from that moment its action becomes vigorous—that is, its course towards the center which attracts it, which infinitely surpasses the velocity of any other movement.

It is action then, but an action so noble, so peaceful, so tranquil, that it seems to the soul as though it were not acting at all; because it rests, as it were, naturally. When a wheel is only turning with a moderate speed, it can easily be distinguished; but when it goes quickly, no part of it can be distinctly seen. So the soul which remains at rest in God has an action infinitely noble and exalted, yet very peaceful. The greater its peace, the greater is its velocity, because it is abandoned to the Spirit, who moves it and makes it act. This Spirit is God Himself, who draws us, and in drawing makes us run to Him, as the Bride well knew when she said, "Draw me, we will run" (Cant. 1:4). Draw me, O my Divine Center, by my inmost heart: my powers and my sensibilities will run at Thy attraction! This attraction alone is a balm which heals me, and a perfume which draws. "We will run," she says, "because of the savor of Thy good ointments." This attracting virtue is very strong but the soul follows it very gladly; and as it is equally strong and sweet, it attracts by its strength and delights by its sweetness.

The Bride says, "Draw me, we will run." She speaks of herself, and to herself: "Draw me;" there is the unity of the object which is attracted: "We will run;" there is the correspondence of all the powers and sensibilities which follow in the train of the center of the heart.

It is not then a question of remaining in idleness, but of acting in dependence upon the Spirit of God, who animates us, since it is in Him that "we live, and move, and have our being" (Acts 17:23). This calm dependence upon the Spirit of God is absolutely necessary, and causes the soul in a short time to attain the simplicity and unity in which it was created. It was created one and simple, like God. In order, then, to answer the end of our creation, we must quit the multiplicity of our own actions, to enter into the simplicity and unity of God, in whose image we were created (Gen. 1:27). The Spirit of God is "one only," "yet manifold" (Wisdom of Solomon 7:22), and its unity does not prevent its multiplicity. We enter into God's unity when we are united to His Spirit, because then we have the same Spirit that He has; and we are multiplied outwardly, as regards His dispositions, without leaving the unity.

So that, as God acts infinitely, and we are of one spirit with

Him, we act much more than we could do by our own action. We must suffer ourselves to be guided by Wisdom. This "Wisdom" is more moving than any motion (Wisdom of Solomon 7:24). Let us, then, remain in dependence upon His action, and our action will be vigorous indeed.

"All things were made by (the Word); and without Him was not anything made that was made" (John 1:3). God, in creating us, created us in His image, after His likeness (Gen. 1:26). He gave to us the Spirit of the Word by the breath of life (Gen. 2:7), which He breathed into us when we were created in the image of God, by the participation of the life of the Word, who is the image of His Father. Now this life is one, simple, pure, intimate, and fruitful.

The devil having disfigured this beautiful image, it became necessary that this same Word, whose breath had been breathed into us at our creation, should come to restore it. It was necessary that it should be He, because He is the image of the Father; and a defaced image cannot be repaired by its own action, but by the action of him who seeks to restore it. Our action then should be, to put ourselves into a position to suffer the action of God, and to allow the Word to retrace His image in us. An image, if it could move, would by its movement prevent the sculptor's perfecting it. Every movement of our own hinders the work of the Heavenly Sculptor, and produces false features.

We must then remain silent, and only move as He moves us. Jesus Christ has life in Himself (John 5:26), and He must communicate life to all who live.

That this action is the most noble cannot be denied. Things are only of value as the principle in which they originate is noble, grand, and elevated. Actions committed by a divine principle are divine actions; whereas the actions of the creature, however good they may appear, are human actions or at best they are virtuous actions, if they are done with the help of grace.

Jesus says that He has life in Himself; all other beings have but a borrowed life, but the Word has life in Himself; and as He is communicative, He desires to communicate this life to men. We must then give place to this life, that it may flow in us, which can only be done by evacuation, and the loss of the life of Adam and of our own action, as St Paul assures us: "If any man be in Christ, he is a new creature: old things are passed away; behold all things are become new" (2 Cor. 5:17). This can only be brought about by the death of ourselves and of our own action, that the action of God may be substituted for it. We do not profess, then, to be without action, but only to act in dependence upon the Spirit of God, suffering His action to take the place of our own. Jesus shows us this in the gospel. Martha did good things, but because she did them of her own spirit, Christ reproved her for them. The spirit of man is turbulent and boisterous; therefore it does little, though it appears to do much. "Martha, Martha," said Jesus, "thou art careful and troubled about many things; but one thing is needful; and Mary hath chosen that good part, which shall not be taken away from her" (Luke 10:41, 42).

What had she chosen, this Magdalene? Peace, tranquility, and repose. She apparently ceased to act, that she might be moved by the Spirit of God; she ceased to live, that Christ might live in her.

This is why it is so necessary to renounce ourselves and all our own works to follow Jesus; for we cannot follow Him unless we are animated with His Spirit. In order that the Spirit of Christ may dwell in us, our own spirit must give place to Him. "He that is joined to the Lord," says St Paul, "is one spirit" (1 Cor. 6:17). "It is good for me to draw near to God: I have put my trust in the Lord God" (Ps. 78:28). What is this "drawing near"? It is the beginning of union.

Union has its beginning, its continuation, its completion, and its consummation. The commencement of union is an inclination towards God. When the soul is converted in the manner I have described, it has an inclination to its center, and a strong tendency to union: this tendency is the commencement. Then it adheres, which happens when it approaches nearer to God; then it is united to Him, and finally becomes one with Him—that is, it becomes one spirit with Him; and it is then that this spirit, which proceeded from God, returns to Him as its end.

It is, then, necessary that we should enter this way, which is the divine motion, and the Spirit of Jesus Christ. St Paul says, "If any man have not the Spirit of Christ, he is none of His" (Rom. 8:9). To be Christ's, then, we must suffer ourselves to be filled with His Spirit, and emptied of our own: our hearts must be evacuated. St Paul, in the same place, proves to us the necessity of this divine motion: he says, "As many as are led by the Spirit of God, they are the sons of God" (Rom. 8:14).

The divinely-imparted Spirit is the Spirit of divine sonship; therefore, the same apostle continues, "Ye have not received the spirit of bondage again to fear; but ye have received the spirit of adoption, whereby we cry, Abba, Father" (Rom. 8:15). This spirit is no other than the Spirit of Christ, by whom we participate in His Sonship; and this "Spirit itself beareth witness with our spirit that we are the sons of God."

As soon as the soul leaves itself to be moved by the Spirit of God, it experiences the witness of this divine sonship; and this witness serves the more to increase its joy, as it makes it know that it is called to the liberty of the sons of God, and that the spirit it has received is not a spirit of bondage, but of liberty.

The Spirit of the divine motion is so necessary for all things, that Paul founds this necessity upon our ignorance of the things that we ask for. "The Spirit," he says, "helpeth our infirmities; for we know not what we should pray for as we ought; but the Spirit itself maketh intercession for us, with groanings which cannot be uttered." This is conclusive: if we do not know what to pray for, nor how to ask as we ought for what is necessary for us, and if it is needful that the Spirit who is in us, to whose motion we abandon ourselves, should ask it for us, ought we not to leave Him to do it? He does it "with groanings which cannot be uttered."

This Spirit is the Spirit of the Word, who is always heard, as He says Himself: "I know that Thou hearest me always" (John 11:42). If we leave it to the Spirit within us to ask and to pray, we shall always be answered. Why so? O great apostle, mystic teacher, so deeply taught in the inner life! teach us why. "It is," he adds, "because He that searcheth the hearts knoweth what is the mind of the Spirit, because He maketh intercession for the saints according to the will of God;" that is to say, this Spirit only asks that which it is God's will to give. It is God's will that we should be saved and that we should be perfect. He asks, then, for all that is necessary to our perfection. Why, after this, should we be burdened with superfluous cares, and be wearied in the greatness of our way, without ever saying, There is no hope in ourselves, and therefore resting in God? God Himself invites us to cast all our care upon Him, and He complains, in inconceivable goodness, that we employ our strength, our riches, and our treasure, in countless exterior things, although there is so little joy to be found in them all. "Wherefore do ye spend money for that which is not bread, and your labor for that which satisfieth not? Hearken diligently unto me, and eat ye that which is good, and let your soul delight itself in fatness" (Isa. 55:2).

Oh, if it were known what happiness there is in thus hearkening unto God, and how the soul is strengthened by it! All flesh must be silent before the Lord (see Zech. 2:13). All self-effort must cease when He appears. In order still further to induce us to abandon ourselves to Him without reserve, God assures us that we need fear nothing from such abandonment, because He has a special individual care over each of us. He says, "Can a woman forget her sucking-child, that she should not have compassion on the son of her womb? Yea, she may forget, yet will I not forget thee" (Isa. 49:15). Ah, words full of consolation! Who on hearing them can fear to abandon himself utterly to the guidance of God?

Chapter 17

DISTINCTION BETWEEN EXTERIOR AND INTERIOR ACTIONS

THOSE OF THE SOUL IN THIS CONDITION ARE INTERIOR, BUT HABITUAL, CONTINUED, DIRECT, PROFOUND, SIMPLE, AND IMPERCEPTIBLE — BEING A CONTINUAL SINKING IN THE OCEAN OF DIVINITY — SIMILITUDE OF A VESSEL — HOW TO ACT IN THE ABSENCE OF SENSIBLE SUPPORTS

THE actions of men are either exterior or interior. The exterior are those which appear outwardly, and have a sensible object, possessing neither good nor evil qualities, excepting as they receive them from the interior principle in which they originate. It is not of these that I intend to speak, but only of interior actions, which are those actions of the soul by which it applies itself inwardly to some object, or turns away from some other.

When, being applied to God, I desire to commit an action of a different nature from those which He would prompt, I turn away from God, and I turn towards created things more or less according to the strength or weakness of my action. If, being turned towards the creature, I wish to return to God, I must commit the action of turning away from the creature, and turning towards God; and thus the more perfect is this action, the more complete will be the conversion.

Until I am perfectly converted, I need several actions to turn me towards God. Some are done all at once, others gradually; but my action ought to lead me to turn to God, employing all the strength of my soul for Him, as it is written, "Therefore even now, saith the Lord, turn ye even to me with all your heart" (Joel 2:12). "Thou shalt return unto the Lord thy God ... with all thine heart and with all thy soul" (Deut. 30:2). God only asks for our heart: "My son, give me thy heart, and let thine eyes observe my ways" (Prov. 23:26). To give the heart to God is to have its gaze, its strength, and its vigor all centered in Him, to follow His will. We must, then, after we have applied to God, remain always turned towards Him.

But as the mind of man is weak, and the soul, being accustomed to turn towards earthly things, is easily turned away from God, it must, as soon as it perceives that it is turned towards outward things, resume its former position in God by a simple act of return to Him.

And as several repeated acts form a habit, the soul contracts a habit of conversion, and from action it passes to a habitual condition.

The soul, then, must not seek by means of any efforts or works of its own to come near to God; this is seeking to perform one action by means of others, instead of by a simple action remaining attached to God alone.

If we believe that we must commit no actions, we are mistaken, for we are always acting; but each one must act according to his degree.

I will endeavor to make this point clear, as, for want of understanding it, it presents a difficulty to many Christians.

There are passing and distinct actions, and continued actions; direct acts and reflected acts. All cannot perform the first, and all are not in a condition to perform the others. The first actions should be committed by those who are turned away from God. They ought to turn to Him by a distinct action, more or less strong according to their distance from Him.

By a continued action I understand that by which the soul is completely turned towards its God by a direct action, which it does not renew, unless it has been interrupted, but which exists. The soul being altogether turned in this way, is in love, and remains there: "And he that dwelleth in love, dwelleth in God" (1 John iv. 16). Then the soul may be said to be in a habitual act, resting even in this action. But its rest is not idle, for it has an action always in force, viz., a gentle sinking in God, in which God attracts it more and more strongly; and, following this attraction, and resting in love, it sinks more and more in this love, and has an action infinitely stronger, more vigorous, and more prompt, than that action which forms only the return. Now the soul which is in this profound and strong action, being turned towards its God, does not perceive this action, because it is direct, and not reflex; so that persons in this condition, not knowing how rightly to describe it, say that they have no action. But they are mistaken; they were never more active. It would be better to say they do not distinguish any action, than that they do not commit any.

The soul does not act of itself, I admit; but it is drawn, and it follows the attracting power. Love is the weight which sinks it, as a person who falls in the sea sinks, and would sink to infinity if the sea were infinite; and without perceiving its sinking, it would sink to the most profound depths with an incredible speed. It is, then, incorrect to say that no actions are committed. All commit actions, but all do not commit them in the same manner; and the abuse arises from the fact, that those who know that action is inevitable wish it to be distinct and sensible. But sensible action is for beginners, and the other for those more advanced. To stop with the first would be to deprive ourselves of the last; and to wish to commit the last before having passed the first would be an equal abuse.

Everything must be done in its season; each state has its commencement, its progress, and its end. There is no act which has not its beginning. At first we must work with effort, but afterwards we enjoy the fruit of our labor.

When a vessel is in the harbor, the sailors have a difficulty in bringing it into the open sea; but once there, they easily turn it in the direction in which they wish to navigate. So, when the soul is in sin, it needs an effort to drag it out; the cords which bind it must be loosened; then, by means of strong and vigorous action, it must be drawn within itself, little by little leaving the harbor, and being turned within, which is the place to which its voyage should be directed.

When the vessel is thus turned, in proportion as it advances in the sea, it leaves the land behind it, and the further it goes from the land, the less effort is needed to carry it along. At last it begins to sail gently, and the vessel goes on so rapidly that the oars become useless. What does the pilot do then? He is contented with spreading the sails and sitting at the helm.

Spreading the sails is simply laying ourselves before God, to be moved by His Spirit. Sitting at the helm is preventing our heart from leaving the right way, rowing it gently, and leading it according to the movement of the Spirit of God, who gradually takes possession of it, as the wind gradually fills the sails, and impels the vessel forward. So long as the vessel sails before the wind, the mariners rest from their labor. They voyage farther in an hour, while they rest in this manner and leave the ship to be carried along by the wind, than they would in a much longer time by their own efforts; and if they wished to row, besides the fatigue which would result from it, their labor would be useless, and would only serve to retard the vessel.

This is the conduct we should pursue in our inner life, and in acting thus we shall advance more in a short time by the Divine guidance, than we ever could do by our own efforts. If only you will try this way, you will find it the easiest possible.

When the wind is contrary, if the wind and the tempest are violent, the anchor must be thrown in the sea to stop the vessel. This anchor is trust in God and hope in His goodness, waiting in patience for the tempest to cease, and for a favorable wind to return, as David did: "I waited patiently for the Lord," he says, "and He inclined unto me" (Ps. 40:1).

Chapter 18

THE DRYNESS OF PREACHERS

AND THE VARIOUS EVILS WHICH ARISE FROM THEIR FAILING TO TEACH HEART-PRAYER — EXHORTATION TO PASTORS TO LEAD PEOPLE TOWARDS THIS FORM OF PRAYER, WITHOUT AMUSING THEM WITH STUDIED AND METHODICAL DEVOTION

IF all those who are working for the conquest of souls sought to win them by the heart, leading them first of all to prayer and to the inner life, they would see many and lasting conversions. But so long as they only address themselves to the outside, and instead of drawing people to Christ by occupying their hearts with Him, they only give them a thousand precepts for outward observances, they will see but little fruit, and that will not be lasting.

When once the heart is won, other defects are easily corrected. This is why God particularly asks for the heart. By this means alone would be prevented the drunkenness, blasphemy, lewdness, enmity, and robbery which are prevalent in the world. Jesus Christ would reign universally, and the Church everywhere would be revived.

Error only takes possession of the soul in the absence of faith and prayer. If men could be taught to believe simply and to pray, instead of disputing amongst themselves, they would be gently led to Christ.

Oh, how inestimable is the loss of those who neglect the inner life! Oh, what an account will they have to render to God who have the charge of souls, for not having discovered this hidden treasure to all those whom they serve in the ministry of the Word!

The excuse given is that there is danger in this way, or that ignorant people are incapable of spiritual things. The oracle of truth assures us that God has hid these things from the wise and prudent, and has revealed them to babes. And what danger can there be in walking in the only true way, which is Jesus Christ, in giving ourselves to Him, looking to Him continually, putting all our trust in His grace, and tending, with all the forces of our souls, to His pure love?

Far from the simple ones being incapable of this perfection, they are the most suitable for it, because they are more docile, more humble, and more innocent; and as they do not reason, they are not so attached to their own light. Having no science, they more readily suffer themselves to be guided by the Spirit of God: while others who are blind in their own sufficiency resist the divine inspiration.

God tells us, too, that it is to the simple He gives understanding by the entrance of His Word (Ps. 119:130). "The testimony of the Lord is sure, making wise the simple" (Ps. 19:7). "The Lord preserveth the simple: I was brought low, and He helped me" (Ps. 116:6).

O ye who have the oversight of souls! see that you do not prevent the little ones from going to Christ. His words to His disciples were, "Suffer little children to come unto me, and forbid them not; for of such is the kingdom of God" (Luke 28:16). Jesus only said this to His disciples, because they wished to keep the children away from Him. Often the remedy is applied to the body, when the disease is at the heart. The reason why we have so little success in seeking to reform men, is that we direct our efforts to the outside, and all that we can do there soon passes off. But if we were to give them first the key of the interior, the outside would be reformed at once with a natural facility.

And this is very easy. To teach them to seek God in their heart, to think of Him, to return to Him when they find they have turned away, to do all and suffer all for the sake of pleasing Him—this is to direct them to the source of all grace, and to make them find there all that is necessary for their sanctification. O you who serve souls! I conjure you to put them first of all into this way, which is Jesus Christ; and it is He who conjures you to do this by the blood He has shed for the souls He confides to your care. "Speak to the heart of Jerusalem" (Isa. 40:2, marg.) O dispensers of His grace, preachers of His Word, ministers of sacraments! establish His kingdom; and, in order to establish it truly, make it reign over hearts. For as it is the heart alone which can oppose His empire, it is by the subjection of the heart that His sovereignty is most honored. Alas! we seek to make studied prayers; and by wishing to arrange them too much, we render them impossible.

We have alienated children from the best of Fathers, in seeking to teach them a polished language. Go, poor children, and speak to your Heavenly Father in your natural language: however uncultivated it may be, it is not so to Him. A father loves best the speech which is put in disorder by love and respect, because he sees that it comes from the heart: it is more to him than a dry harangue, vain and unfruitful though well studied. Oh, how certain glances of love charm and ravish Him! They express infinitely more than all language and reason. By wishing to teach how to love — Love Himself with method, much of this love has been lost. Oh! it is not necessary to teach the art of loving. The language of love is barbarous to him who does not love; and we cannot learn to love God better than by loving Him.

The Spirit of God does not need our arrangements; He takes shepherds at His pleasure to make them prophets; and, far from closing the palace of prayer to any, as it is imagined, He leaves the doors open to all, and Wisdom is ordered to cry in the public places, "Whoso is simple, let him turn in hither: as for him that wanteth understanding, she saith to him, Come, eat of my bread, and drink of the wine which I have mingled" (Prov. 9:4, 5). Did not Christ thank His Father that He had hidden these things from the wise and prudent, and had revealed them to babes? (Matt. 11:25.)

Chapter 19

AFTER THE PRECEDING WAYS, THERE REMAINS AN AFTER WAY

PREPARATORY TO DIVINE UNION, IN WHICH WISDOM AND JUSTICE MAKE THE PASSIVE PURIFICATION OF THE SOUL, ALL WHICH IS TREATED IN DETAIL IN THE FOLLOWING TREATISE, ENTITLED "SPIRITUAL TORRENTS."

IT is impossible to attain divine union by the way of meditation alone, or even by the affections, or by any luminous or understood prayer. There are several reasons. These are the principal.

First, according to Scripture, "No man shall see God and live" (Exod. 33:20). Now all discursive exercises of prayer, or even of active contemplation, regarded as an end, and not as a preparation for the passive, are exercises of life by which we cannot see God, that is, become united to Him. All that is of man, and of his own industry, however noble and elevated it may be, must die.

St John tells us that "there was silence in heaven." Heaven represents the depths and center of the soul, where all must be in silence when the majesty of God appears. All that belongs to our own efforts, or to ourselves in any way, must be destroyed, because nothing is opposed to God but appropriation, and all the malignity of man is in this appropriation, which is the source of his evil; so that the more a soul loses its appropriation, the more it becomes pure.

Secondly, in order to unite two things so opposed as the purity of God and the impurity of the creature, the simplicity of God and the multiplicity of the creature, God must operate alone; for this can never be done by the effort of the creature, since two things cannot be united unless there is some relation or resemblance between them, as an impure metal would never unite with one that was pure and refined.

What does God do then? He sends before Him His own Wisdom, as fire will be sent upon the earth to consume by its activity all the impurity that is there. Fire consumes all things, and nothing resists its activity. It is the same with Wisdom; it consumes all impurity in the creature, to prepare him for divine union.

This impurity, so opposed to union, is appropriation and activity. Appropriation, because it is the source of the real impurity which can never be united to essential purity; as the sun's rays may touch the mud but cannot unite with it. Activity, because God being in an infinite repose, in order that the soul may be united to Him, it must participate in His repose, without which there can be no union, because of the dissemblance; and to unite two things, they must be in a proportionate rest.

It is for this reason that the soul can only attain divine union by the rest of its will; and it can only be united to God when it is in a central rest and in the purity of its creation.

To purify the soul God makes use of wisdom as fire is used for the purification of gold. It is certain that gold can only be purified by fire, which gradually consumes all that is earthly and foreign, and separates it from the gold. It is not sufficient that the earth should be changed into gold; it is necessary that the fire should melt and dissolve it, to remove from it all that is earthly; and this gold is put in the fire so many times that it loses its impurity, and all necessity of purification. Then it is fit to be employed in the most excellent workmanship.

And if this gold is impure in the end, it is because it has contracted fresh defilement by coming in contact with other bodies. But this impurity is only superficial, and does not prevent its being used; whereas its former impurity was hidden within it, and, as it were, identified with its nature.

In addition to this, you will remark that gold of an inferior degree of purity cannot mix with that of a superior purity. The one must contract the impurity of the other, or else impart its own purity to it. Put a refined gold with an unrefined one, what can the goldsmith ever do with it? He will have all the impurity taken from the second piece, that it may be able to mix with the first. This is what St Paul tells us, that "the fire shall try every man's work of what sort it is;" he adds, that if any man's work should be found to deserve burning, he should be saved "so as by fire" (1 Cor. 3:13, 15). That means, that though there are some works which are good, and which God receives, yet, so that he who has done them may be pure, they too must pass through the fire, in order that all appropriation, that is, all that was his own, may be taken from them. God will judge our righteousness, because "by the deeds of the law there shall no flesh be justified," but by "the righteousness of God, which is by faith" (Rom. 3:20, 22).

This being understood, I say that, in order that man may be united to his God, wisdom and divine justice, like a pitiless and devouring fire, must take from him all appropriation, all that is terrestrial, carnal, and of his own activity; and having taken all this from him, they must unite him to God.

This is never brought about by the labors of the creature; on the contrary, it even causes him regret, because, as I have said, man so loves what is his own, and is so fearful of its destruction, that if God did not accomplish it Himself, and by His own authority, man would never consent to it.

It will be objected to this, that God never deprives man of his liberty, and that therefore he can always resist God; for which reason I ought not to say that God acts absolutely, without the consent of man. In explanation I say, that it is sufficient that man should give a passive consent, that he may have entire and full liberty; because having at the beginning given himself to God, that He may do as He will both with him and in him, he gave from that time an active and general assent to all that God might do. But when God destroys, burns, and purifies, the soul does not see that all this is for its advantage; it rather believes the contrary: and as at first the fire seems to tarnish the gold, so this operation seems to despoil the soul of its purity. So that if an active and explicit consent were required, the soul would find a difficulty in giving it, and often would not give it. All that it does is to remain in a passive contentment, enduring this operation as well as it can, being neither able nor willing to prevent it.

God then so purifies this soul of all natural, distinct, and perceived operations, that at last He makes it more and more conformed to Himself, and then uniform, raising the passive capacity of the creature, enlarging it and ennobling it, though in a hidden and unperceived manner, which is termed mystical. But in all these operations the soul must concur passively, and in proportion as the working of God becomes stronger, the soul must continually yield to Him, until He absorbs it altogether. We do not say, then, as some assert, that there must be no action; since, on the contrary, this is the door; but only that we must not remain in it, seeing that man should tend towards the perfection of his end, and that he can never reach it without quitting the first means, which, though they were necessary to introduce him into the way, would greatly hinder him afterwards, if he attached himself obstinately to them. This is what Paul said, "I forget those things which are behind, and reach forth unto those things which are before; I press toward the mark" (Phil. 3:13, 14).

Should we not consider a person destitute of reason who, after undertaking a journey, stopped at the first inn, because he was assured that several had passed it, that a few had lodged there, and that the landlord lived there? What the soul is required to do, then, is to advance towards its end, to take the shortest road, not to stop at the first point, and, following the advice of St Paul, to suffer itself to be "led by the Spirit of God" (Rom. 8:14), who will lead it to the end for which it was created, which is the enjoyment of God.

It is well known that the sovereign good is God; that essential blessedness consists in union with God, and that this union cannot be the result of our own efforts, since God only communicates Himself to the soul according to its capacity. We cannot be united to God without passivity and simplicity; and this union being bliss, the way which leads to it must be the best, and there can be no risk in walking in it.

This way is not dangerous. If it were, Christ would not have represented it as the most perfect and necessary of all ways. All can walk in it; and as all are called to blessedness, all are called to the enjoyment of God, both in this life and in that which is to come, since the enjoyment of God is blessedness. I say the enjoyment of God Himself, not of His gifts, which can never impart essential blessedness, not being able fully to satisfy the soul, which is so constituted that even the richest gifts of God cannot thoroughly content it. The desire of God is to give Himself to us, according to the capacity with which He has endowed us; and yet we fear to leave ourselves to God! We fear to possess Him, and to be prepared for divine union!

You say, we must not bring ourselves to this condition. I agree to that; but I say too, that no one ever could bring himself to it, since no man could ever unite himself to God by his own efforts, and God Himself must do the work.

You say that some pretend to have attained it. I say that this state cannot be feigned, any more than a man dying of hunger can for any length of time pretend to be satisfied. It will soon be known whether or no men have attained this end.

Since, then, none can arrive at the end unless he be brought there, it is not a question of introducing people to it, but of showing them the way which leads to it, and begging them not to rest in those practices which must be relinquished at God's command.

Would it not be cruelty to show a fountain to a thirsty man, and then hold him bound, and prevent his going to it, leaving him to die of thirst? That is what is being done now. Let us all be agreed both as to the way and the end. The way has its commencement, its progress, and its terminus. The more we advance towards the terminus, the farther we go from the commencement; and it is impossible to reach the terminus but by constantly going farther from the starting-point, being unable to go from one place to another without passing through all that comes between them: this is incontestable.

Oh, how blind are the majority of men, who pride themselves upon their learning and talent!

O Lord! how true it is that Thou hast hidden Thy secrets from the wise and prudent, and hast revealed them unto babes!

Summary:

* Meditate on Scripture – digest it before you go on to the next. You don't get nourished until you chew and swallow and digest.
* Praying the Word will help keep you from distractions.
* Don't jump from subject to subject.
* Enter His presence through His Word.
* Slow down – go one line at a time of the Lord's Prayer.
* Start with quiet moments, where you don't seek anything but to love Him.
* God desires to impart Himself, but also conceals Himself for a purpose at times; await patiently, in abandonment and contentment. Learn to wait with sighs of love.
* Abandonment is the key to the inner court. Don't listen to other confusing voices of natural reason; great faith produces great abandonment. Cast off selfish cares, Matt 6:34, Prov 3:6; 37:5, Prov 16:3. Abandonment and the cross go hand in hand; when God comes into your life He brings all His goodness.
* Your soulish desires still give energy to your senses. Your senses stimulate your passions. The more activity you begin to overcome, this self nature you redirect to harsh feelings about yourself and stir up more passions.
* The only genuine means of bringing about change is through inward means. Commit yourself wholly into hands of loving God; the nearer your spirit draws to God the further you become separated from soulish demands. Place your focus on getting to know God and abandon all to God to be perfected. Learn to main steadfast in attention to God.
* Your imagination will continually supply you with danger of falling in excess activity of dying to self. But God will teach you to only follow His promptings. Rewards are great; you will find yourself constantly relying on God.

www.ingramcontent.com/pod-product-compliance
Lightning Source LLC
Chambersburg PA
CBHW020427010526
44118CB00010B/462